Step-by-Step
MS-DOS 5.0

Step-by-Step
MS-DOS 5.0

Alan Balfe

NEWTECH

Newtech
An imprint of Butterworth-Heinemann Ltd
Linacre House, Jordan Hill, Oxford OX2 8DP

PART OF REED INTERNATIONAL BOOKS

OXFORD   LONDON   BOSTON
MUNICH   NEW DELHI   SINGAPORE   SYDNEY
TOKYO   TORONTO   WELLINGTON

First published 1992

© Alan Balfe 1992

All rights reserved. No part of this publication may be reproduced in any material form (including photocopying or storing in any medium by electronic means and whether or not transiently or incidentally to some other use of this publication) without the written permission of the copyright holder except in accordance with the provisions of the Copyright, Designs and Patents Act 1988 or under the terms of a licence issued by the Copyright Licensing Agency Ltd, 90 Tottenham Court Road, London W1P 9HE, England. Applications for the copyright holder's written permission to reproduce any part of this publication should be addressed to the publishers.

NOTICE

The authors and the publishers have used their best efforts to prepare this book, including the computer examples contained in it. The computer examples have been tested. The authors and publishers make no warranty, implicit or explicit, about the documentation. The authors and the publishers will not be liable under any circumstances for any direct or indirect damages arising from any use, direct or indirect, of the documentation or the computer examples contained in this book.

British Library Cataloguing in Publication Data
A CIP catalogue record for this book is available from the publishers

ISBN 0-7506-0471-9

Printed and bound in Great Britain by
Biddle Ltd, Guildford and King's Lynn
Layout and Design by GLM Ltd., Mountsorrel, Loughborough,
Leicestershire LE12 7HH
Main body text Palatino 10 Point on 15 Point leading

Dedication

For Steve and Jane,
In thanks for bacon butties and listening endlessly!

Trademarks

MS-DOS, Microsoft, Windows, Microsoft Excel, GW-BASIC, QBASIC, XENIX and the MicroSoft Logo are all registered trademarks of the Microsoft Corporation Ltd.
AST is a registered trademark of AST Research Inc.
AT, IBM and PS/2, PC/XT and Proprinter are registered trademarks of International Business Machines Corporation.
AT&T is a registered trademark of American Telephone and Telegraph Company.
Compaq is a registered trademark of Compaq Computer Products.
Epson is a registered trademark of Epson Corporation.
Hewlett-Packard, HP, DeskJet, LaserJet, PaintJet, ThinkJet and Vectra are registered trademarks of Hewlett-Packard Company.
Intel is a registered trademark of Intel Corporation.
PageMaker is a registered trademark of Aldus Corporation Inc.
Philips is a registered trademark of Philips International B.V.
PostScript is a registered trademark of Adobe Systems Inc.
Toshiba is a registered trademark of Kabushiki Kaisha Toshiba.
Tulip is a registered trademark of Tulip Computers International B.V.
Weitek is a registered trademark of Weitek Corporation.
WordStar is a registered trademark of WordStar International Corporation.
Wyse is a registered trademark of Wyse Technology.
Zenith is a registered trademark of Zenith Radio Corporation.

Contents

Part One Introduction

History of MS-DOS 14
MS-DOS Versions 16
Notational Conventions 19
Assumptions 21
Before you start 23

Part Two Background

What is a program? 28
Program types 30
File types 33
ASCII files 35
Allowable filenames 37
Reserved filenames 39
Disk terms 43
Disk storage 47
Physical and Logical 51
Directories 55
Directory Structure 59
Disk areas 64

Contents

Part Three Resources

Hardware 68
Chips 73
Booting up 78
Internal or External 82
Devices 84
Memory 87

Part Four Installation

Getting ready 90
Installing MS-DOS 5.0 94
Tidying up 98

Part Five Configuration

Using memory 100
Using resources 104
Editing files 106
Freeing memory 114
Using 8 Mb of RAM 118

Contents

Part Six Commands

Types of commands	122
ANSI.SYS	124
APPEND.EXE	126
ASSIGN.COM	130
ATTRIB.EXE	133
AUTOEXEC.BAT	137
BACKUP.EXE	139
BREAK	144
BUFFERS	146
CALL	149
CHCP	151
CHDIR	153
CHKDSK.EXE	156
CLS	159
COMMAND.COM	160
COMP.EXE	162
CONFIG.SYS	165
COPY	167
COUNTRY.SYS	171
CTTY	174
DATE	176
DEBUG.EXE	178
DEL	181
DELOLDOS.EXE	183
DEVICE	184
DIR	187
DIRCMD	191
DISKCOMP.COM	192
DISKCOPY.COM	195

9

Contents

DISPLAY.SYS	198
DOS	200
DOSKEY.COM	202
DOSSHELL.COM	206
DRIVER.SYS	208
DRIVPARM	210
ECHO	212
EDIT.COM	214
EDLIN.EXE	216
EGA.SYS	219
EMM386.EXE	220
EXE2BIN.EXE	225
EXIT	227
EXPAND.EXE	228
FASTOPEN.EXE	230
FC.EXE	233
FCBS	236
FDISK.EXE	237
FILES	240
FIND.EXE	242
FOR	244
FORMAT.COM	246
GOTO	250
GRAFTABL.COM	251
GRAPHICS.COM	254
HELP.EXE	257
HIMEM.SYS	258
IF	261
INSTALL	263
IO.SYS	265
JOIN.EXE	266
KEYB.COM	268

Contents

LABEL.EXE	272
LASTDRIVE	274
LOADFIX.COM	276
LOADHIGH	277
MEM.EXE	279
MIRROR.COM	282
MKDIR	285
MODE.COM	287
MORE.COM	294
MSHERC.COM	296
NLSFUNC.EXE	297
PATH	298
PAUSE	300
PRINT.EXE	301
PRINTER.SYS	303
PROMPT	305
QBASIC.EXE	308
RAMDRIVE.SYS	310
RECOVER.EXE	313
REM	315
RENAME	316
REPLACE.EXE	318
RESTORE.EXE	321
RMDIR	324
SET	326
SETVER.EXE	328
SHARE.EXE	331
SHELL	333
SHIFT	335
SMARTDRV.SYS	337
SORT.EXE	339
STACKS	342

Contents

SUBST.EXE 344
SWITCHES 347
SYS.COM 348
TIME 350
TEMP 352
TREE.COM 354
TYPE 356
UNDELETE.EXE 358
UNFORMAT.COM 361
VER 363
VERIFY 364
VOL 366
XCOPY.EXE 367

Appendices

Text Editor 373
Extended ASCII Characters 383

Index 385

Part One
Introduction

History of MS-DOS

A computer system is a collection of electronic circuits connected to a range of other devices, such as a monitor, disk drive, keyboard, etc. Supply it with an electric current, however, and then it sits there doing nothing - unless, that is, you supply it with an operating system. This is a collection of software which controls all the elements of the system and allows them to communicate with each other. Without the operating system the computer is just so much junk. But once the system is in place you have a machine which can save you enormous amounts of time and trouble. The relationship between the software and hardware is a symbiotic one - neither will function without the other, but when combined into a single organism they become greater than the sum of the parts. The best known operating system is MS-DOS - Microsoft Disk Operating System. This is 'fitted' to every PC, XT and AT that is marketed around the world. The history and development of the operating system is a story unto itself.

Computers have a relatively short history, in terms of the lifetime of Mankind. The first electronic computer was developed and built during World War Two, but it was a huge, cumbersome, slow device which required a veritable army of technicians to keep it working properly. Since that time, the machines have got smaller and smaller; first the Transistor and then the Integrated Circuit have reduced the size and running costs while increasing the performance and power of the machines. In the late 1970's the size of computers had reduced to such an extent that it was possible to get the whole thing, bar the monitor, into a box not much larger than a portable typewriter. However, business users remained tied to the large mainframe machines that they had been using for a generation - albeit with modifications and increased performance. The desk top machines used an operating system called CP/M - an acronym for Control Program and Microprocessors. This worked very well on computers

History of MS-DOS

which used 8-bit chips. (This simply means that the machine moved data about in chunks of 8 Binary Digits at a time.) As 8-bits is the minimum space any single character can occupy this meant that the machine could only operate with one alphanumeric character each clock cycle. But then the Intel Corporation developed a 16-bit chip and CP/M was suddenly redundant.

16-bit chips are not just twice as fast as their earlier cousins, the figure is much nearer to three times as quick due to other factors. What was needed was a new operating system - especially when IBM announced its intention to develop and market a desk top computer that used the new chip. They asked Digital Research, the company responsible for CP/M, for a new operating system but then decided not to use it for some reason. This left them in a quandary - the machine was well on the way to being finished but there was no suitable operating system for it.

Meanwhile, there was, and still is, a company called Seattle Computer Products. They had developed an operating system for 16-bit chips called Q-DOS but then found they did not have the resources to complete the development and marketing of it. So they sold the product, its copyright and development rights to another company called Microsoft. This company was well known in the computer industry for its programming languages, such as BASIC, and while it was much larger than Seattle Computer Products it was still a small company. Microsoft took Q-DOS, reworked some of it, revamped other parts and added extra bits and then renamed it MS-DOS. This was then offered to IBM who promptly accepted it and used it on their new machine which was launched in August 1980. Since then the computer, called the IBM Personal Computer, and MS-DOS have gone from strength to strength. Microsoft is now the biggest software company in the world as a direct result.

MS-DOS Versions

Since its inception MS-DOS has been upgraded and improved a number of times. Generally these rewrites have been done to take account of new hardware advances but occasionally they are done to remove bugs which have been introduced into the operating system as the result of a previous rewrite. Traditionally, all computer software is sequentially numbered and this follows very strict rules.

The Version number consists of two or three digits separated by a full stop, e.g. 1.0, 2.11, 3.21. The digit before the full stop is the actual Version number, while the remaining digits refer to the upgrade of that Version. The Version number changes only whenever there is a major rewrite of the software, adding extra capabilities or dramatic improvements. The rewrite digits change whenever a Version has to be debugged to correct minor errors. This ruling about Version numbers applies to all computer software, not just MS-DOS. The main MS-DOS versions were and are:

> The original operating system, as used on the first IBM PC, was Version 1.0 and it did not last very long. With the advent of double sided floppy disk drives it was necessary to improve MS-DOS so that it could handle the new disks. However this was not a major rewrite and so was released as Version 1.10.
>
> Version 2.0 came about as the result of the advent of hard disk drives - at the time of the release of the original PC, hard disk drives existed only for mainframe machines. In addition to improving the system so that it could support the hard disks the operating system was redesigned and improved to make it closer to the XENIX operating system, rather than remaining close to CP/M. This is why you will frequently see commercial software which says 'you must use MS-DOS 2.0 or higher'.

MS-DOS Versions

Version 2.10 was created to allow support for half-height disk drives. The hardware configuration has a fundamental effect on how MS-DOS must operate and so changes from full height to half-height drives necessitated minor rewriting of the operating system. At the same time a number of bugs, which had become apparent in Version 2.0 were corrected. (Generally speaking any software labelled Version n.0 will contain some bugs - this is one of the 'laws' of computing!)

Version 3.0 again came about because of a major hardware change. High capacity floppy disk drives had arrived, i.e. 1.44 Mb instead of 360 Kb, and so Microsoft took the opportunity to perform a major revision of the operating system. A number of the commands were completely rewritten, while others were merely improved.

Version 3.10 added support for a network, in this case MS-NET. Again a number of known bugs were corrected but the operating system did not fundamentally change, hence only the final two digits changed.

Version 3.2 provided support for the IBM Token ring network and the new 3.5-inch floppy disks. This is probably the most widely used version of MS-DOS in the U.K. because it is supplied with every Amstrad 1512 and 1640 machine - and there were an awful lot of them sold.

Version 3.21 corrected some more bugs but otherwise made no changes.

Version 3.30 was another minor rewrite. It provided support for the new high capacity 3.5-inch disks, allowing the machine

MS-DOS Versions

to have and operate four serial ports - previous versions would only allow two. It also included a brand new command, FASTOPEN, and complete rewrites of many other commands. However, the basis of the operating system did not change, hence only the final two digits were changed.

Version 4.0 was the next incarnation of MS-DOS. It included some additional commands, enhanced device drivers and major rewrites of most of the commands - some of which now have additional features. One major benefit of this version was that it would allow you to have hard disk partitions which exceed 32 Mb. Because the standard size of hard disks is constantly increasing this was an important feature. Unfortunately MS-DOS 4.0 has a terrible reputation for being cumbersome, awkward and it is not as bug free as one would like. The result is that not many people use it: certainly given the choice many people will use another version.

MS-DOS 5.0 is the latest version of the operating system and the best yet. It has been released as an upgrade so that any user can go and purchase it from a supplier and then install it on their system. This is a major change of direction for Microsoft as previously MS-DOS was only available to manufacturers and so the only way to get a new version of MS-DOS was to buy a new machine. All that is gone now, you can buy Version 5.0 for as little as £45 - although the recommended price is £69. Considering the major advances that the new version contains it is well worth the price.

Notational Conventions

Throughout this book you will find certain keystrokes which are required to be input to generate specific effects. The following details show how these will appear.

Key Names

The names of the keys will always appear in bold Helvetica as they are written on the keyboard itself. Thus, Escape appears as **Esc**, Control as **Ctrl**, Alternative as **Alt**, Return as **Enter**, etc. Similarly the function keys appear as **F1**, **F2** and so on. Note also that individual letters always appear in upper case because that is the way they are shown on the keyboard.

Key Combinations and Sequences

Where it is necessary for you to press a number of keys together they will appear in the text in bold Helvetica, joined by a hyphen. Thus **Ctrl-K F** means that you hold down **Ctrl** and **K** at the same time, before releasing them and then pressing **F** by itself. **Ctrl-K-F** on the other hand means that you must press all three keys simultaneously.

If the keys are intended to be pressed sequentially they will appear in bold but without the hyphens. Thus **Esc K Enter** means that you first press **Esc**, release it, then press **K** and release it, finally press **Enter** then release that.

Notational Conventions

Cursor Keys

The arrow keys are referred to by their direction of action and appear in bold type: **Up, Down, Left** and **Right**. The remaining cursor keys are shown as they are on the keypad; for example **PgUp** and **Home**. You may use either those keys on the numeric keypad or the cursor keys proper - they both produce the same effects.

Entering Commands

Throughout this book anything that you have to type verbatim will appear in bold. For example, **FORMAT/S** means that you have to enter exactly that as it is written.

Where you are required to supply a word or filename in a command it appears in bold, small capitals enclosed in square brackets. For example, **MD C:\[directory]** means that you type **MD C:** and then a directory name, which you have to supply, but excluding the brackets, before pressing **Enter** to activate the command.

Response to Input

Where the computer displays a message as a result of your actions on the screen these are shown in bold Helvetica as they appear, e.g. **File not found** or **1 File(s) copied**.

Assumptions

While this book makes no assumptions about your experience or expertise in using computers and MS-DOS, it would be helpful if we clarified a couple of points before getting into the book proper. What follows are the definitions of some of the features used within this book. They are included so we both know what we are talking about.

PC

This is an acronym for Personal Computer, i.e. a machine based on an 8088 or 8086 microchip without a hard disk drive. However, throughout the book we shall use the term PC to refer to the entire family of IBM compatible machines, regardless of whether they are using the 80286, 80386SX, 80386 and 80486 chips.

Drives

By default MS-DOS can only handle five drives and so that is all we will consider. On every computer the disk drives are always allocated upper case letters in the following order.

> **A:** The first floppy drive. All PCs have at least one floppy drive and this can be referred to as either Drive-A or Drive-B.
>
> **B:** The second floppy drive. This may not be present on your machine, in which case the A-Drive functions as both Drive-A and Drive-B.
>
> **C:** The primary partition on a hard disk, i.e. the first hard disk drive. MS-DOS prior to Version 4.0 imposed a limit

Assumptions

of 32 Mb for this. Nowadays it can be the actual size of the entire hard disk although there are justifications for still dividing a large capacity drive into a number of logical drives.

D: The second hard disk drive or secondary partition.

E: The next drive or partition.

System Prompt

Contrary to what many people think this is not the flashing cursor that appears on the screen - that is only one part of it. The system prompt shows you the drive you are logged onto, and possibly the sub-directory, followed by the cursor, e.g. **C:>_** or **A:>_**. Throughout this book, except when stated otherwise, the system prompt refers to Drive-C because the vast majority of PC's today include a hard disk.

Using a Floppy Based Machine

If your computer does not have a hard disk you will be limited to using floppy drives. In this case you should substitute **A:** for every occurrence of **C:** in the examples. However to use any of the external commands you must have the necessary files on a floppy disk in the A-Drive.

Before you start

You should never use the master disks that came with your computer - you should always make copies of them and use those. This applies regardless of whether you are using a floppy or hard disk based machine. If you have not yet copied the disks then follow these steps:

1 You need a number of blank floppies, ideally brand new ones that have not been used for anything else, one for each of the master disks. They do not have to be preformatted but they must be the same size and capacity as the master disks. In other words if the master disks are 360 Kb 5.25-inch floppies then you cannot use 3.5-inch ones nor 1.2 Mb ones.

2 Switch on the computer so that it boots from MS-DOS. On a hard disk this normally means you just turn on the machine because the system files are already on the hard disk. Using a floppy based machine means you have to put the master MS-DOS disk into the A-Drive and boot from that. (Boot simply means supplying the machine with power and an operating system.)

3 To make exactly duplicates of the master disks you use a command called DISKCOPY.COM. Place the first master disk into the floppy drive and then enter **DISKCOPY A: A:**. In other words you are going to copy the contents of the disk in Drive-A into Drive-A. This sounds wrong but it does work because MS-DOS prompts you to change the disk at intervals.

Before you start

4   The computer responds with:

>   **Insert SOURCE diskette in drive A:
>   Press any key when ready . . .**

  Make sure that you have the first master disk in the drive and then press any key to begin the copying process.

5   The computer then displays a second message saying:

>   **Copying ?? tracks
>   ?? Sectors/Track, 2 Side(s)**

  as it copies the contents of the disk into the computer memory. It then says:

>   **Insert TARGET diskette into drive A:
>   Press any key when ready . . .**

6   Remove the master disk from the drive and replace it with one of the blank floppies and then press a key. The contents of the computer memory will then be copied onto this disk. If the disk has not been formatted you will also get another message saying **Formatting while copying . . .**

Before you start

7   Depending on the disk size you may then get the same message as under Step 5 above again. Simply follow the steps until you get the final message saying:

   Diskcopy complete
   Copy another diskette (Y/N)?

8   Because you want to copy all the master disks press **Y** - there is no need to press **Enter**. Then run through Steps 4 to 7 again until you have copied all the master disks. When the final disk has been copied press **N**.

9   Write a new label for each of the copied disks. Write the labels before sticking them on. Take the master disks and put them somewhere safe in case you ever need them again. For all normal purposes use the copies you have just made - these are exact duplicates of the original disks.

Entering Commands

From now on within the text you will encounter the phrase '**enter [SOMETHING]**'. This means that you type the **[SOMETHING]** and then press the **Enter** key. You can use either the one marked Enter on the numeric keypad or the one marked Return on the main keyboard - they both have the same effect.

Part Two
Background

What is a program?

Many people confuse program with programme. The former refers specifically to a set of instructions which a computer can interpret and understand. The latter, on the other hand, refers to a list of events which will take place. Both spellings of the word are accepted as standard within their own spheres of influence - even the Oxford English Dictionary agrees. Thus your actions in operating the computer can be considered as a programme, while the computer acts on program instructions. Unfortunately, especially for the new user, the word program is used with all kinds of connotations, e.g. application program. However, this does not alter the basic meaning of the word. A program is simply a series of instructions, written in logical order, which the machine can use. In fact a computer cannot operate with anything other than programs.

The operating system itself consists of three major programs, plus a host of subsidiary ones - the external commands. It is normal practise for various manufacturers to customise MS-DOS so that it works correctly with their machines - although because of the high degree of compatibility this customisation may not be necessary. The main programs are:

IO.SYS

The initial letters of this program refer to Input/Output and that tells you what the program does. It controls the main system devices, the Input/Output peripherals such as the monitor and keyboard. IO.SYS is a hidden file, in other words when you type **DIR** you cannot see it.

What is a program?

MSDOS.SYS

This is the heart of the operating system and it controls the other programs in MS-DOS. Because it interfaces with the other programs MSDOS.SYS is not hardware dependent. This is the major factor that allows MS-DOS to be used on a host of different machines. Like IO.SYS, this program is also hidden from normal view.

COMMAND.COM

This is the third program in MS-DOS, and unlike the other two it is visible. The program acts as the interpreter between you the user, and the rest of the operating system. In fact it is sometimes called a command interpreter or the system shell. Both terms mean the same thing. Basically the program takes the input from you or other programs and turns them into a language that MSDOS.SYS can understand. COMMAND COM is never renamed - at least I have never seen it so - because many application programs depend on finding it.

Program types

Programs in general can be broken down into different types and this is shown by their extensions. There are three main types of programs EXE, COM and BAT. The last one refers to batch files which are covered elsewhere in this book.

EXE is short for Executable and it identifies files with such an extension as a program which MS-DOS can run. Originally an EXE file was one that could exceed a 64 Kb size limit but these days, with improvements in MS-DOS and hardware, you are likely to find this limit no longer applies. The operating system contains the following EXE files:

APPEND	Sets a search route for data files.
ATTRIB	Used to change file attributes.
BACKUP	Allows you to create backup copies of files.
CHKDSK	Used to examine a disk surface or files.
COMP	Compares files.
DEBUG	Used to test and debug program files.
DOSSHELL	Provides a menuing system.
DOSSWAP	Needs with the above - cannot be run alone.
EDLIN	An editor that you either love or hate.
EMM386	A memory manager.
EXE2BIN	Converts an EXE file to binary format.
EXPAND	Used to uncompress MS-DOS 5 files.
FASTOPEN	Speeds disk access time.
FC	Compares files.
FDISK	Used to define disks and partitions.
FIND	Search for text within a file.
HELP	Provides, minimal, help with commands.
JOIN	Adds drives to the path.
LABEL	Used to apply names to disks.
MEM	Displays memory allocations.

Program types

NLSFUNC	Loads country specific data.
PRINT	A print spooler.
QBASIC	A BASIC language interpreter.
RECOVER	Used to recover lost data.
REPLACE	Updates old versions of files.
RESTORE	The compliment to BACKUP.
SETVER	Sets version number reported to programs.
SHARE	Allows file sharing on a network.
SORT	A filter.
SUBST	Treats a directory as a drive.
UNDELETE	A utility supplied with MS-DOS 5.
XCOPY	Copies files and directories.

By definition all EXE are external commands, that is they are not included within the COMMAND.COM and so to use any of them you must have them available on your disk. In addition some of the above programs affect others and so they cannot be used in conjunction.

In the early days of MS-DOS when it was still loosely based on CP/M, i.e. prior to Version 2.0, the operating system had to have two different kinds of files because of the way it was geared. COM files, short for COMMAND, were those not exceeding 64 Kb, EXE files were those above that limit. This no longer really applies but it is customary to name any file that exceeds the 64 Kb limit as EXE. Within MS-DOS there are a number of files which bear the .COM extension:

ASSIGN	Transfers one drive to another.
COMMAND	One of the three major files.
DISKCOMP	Compares the contents of floppy disks.
DISKCOPY	Makes absolute duplicates of floppies.
DOSKEY	Command line editor and macro generator.

Program types

EDIT	A real text editor - at long last.
FORMAT	Makes disks usable by MS-DOS.
GRAFTABL	Used for graphics only.
GRAPHICS	Allows graphics output to the printer.
KEYB	Loads the keyboard program.
MIRROR	A utility that protects disks.
MODE	Configures system drivers.
MORE	A filter.
MOUSE	The mouse device driver.
MSHERC	Driver for Hercules monitors.
SYS	Transfers system files.
TREE	Displays directory structure.
UNFORMAT	Recovers from accidental format.

As with EXE files, the above are external commands and to use any of them you must have them on the disk and accessible to the operating system. MS-DOS also includes a range of device drivers, programs that make peripherals work, and these mainly have an extension of .SYS. These cannot be run by themselves – they have to be installed - usually in the CONFIG.SYS. The extra files are:

ANSI	For displaying certain graphics.
CONFIG	The file you create to customise the system.
COUNTRY	Sets national parameters.
DISPLAY	Used for setting display types.
DRIVER	Used for extra drives.
EGA	Saves and restores EGA monitors.
HIMEM	Allows access to high memory area.
KEYBOARD	Sets national characteristics.
PRINTER	Allows you to set printer options.
RAMDRIVE	Create an electronic disk drive.
SMARTDRV	A disk caching program.

File types

Files are one of the fundamental parts of the computer operating system. Any computer consists of two basic parts, Hardware, which are those items you can physically see and touch, and Software, the program, data and associated files you cannot see other than via the computer. So what exactly is a file? Basically, regardless of its type, it is simply a collection of instructions or information that the computer can operate with, the former are known as programs while the latter are called data files.

Program files are generally specific to the type of computer you are using. For instance, you cannot use a program that was written on a MAC on an IBM-compatible machine or vice versa - except in very special circumstances. The same normally applies to data files: they tend to be distinctive to the machine - although it is much easier to transport data across machines and it is fairly common practise, for example, to translate data from an IBM-compatible machine to an Apple Mac or vice versa.

There are three types of data file:

ASCII files

There are two ASCII files, that is, they are written by the user directly from the keyboard and all they contain are alphanumeric characters. They allow you to set the parameters by which the system operates once the operating system itself is running. The files are the CONFIG.SYS and the AUTOEXEC.BAT. Neither is essential but each is useful.

File types

Document files

These include all the files created by word processors, spreadsheets, databases and what-have-you. Normally such files contain ASCII characters along with a number of control codes that make them specific to the application that produced them. However, a number of application programs are now capable of importing files which were created by another program, e.g. you can import WordStar files into PageMaker - but not vice versa.

Graphic files

These generally contain no ASCII characters whatever and can normally only be viewed by the program which created them or a program which is capable of importing them.

All files are stored on the disk, whether hard or floppy, in a format that the computer can access and use. Whenever you write a file to the disk it will be processed by the operating system and then passed to the drive controller, which is what is actually responsible for writing the file onto the disk.

ASCII files

As well as the program files, IO.SYS, MSDOS.SYS and COMMAND.COM, most computers also contain two other system files - CONFIG.SYS and AUTOEXEC.BAT. Both of these are ASCII files and they allow you to configure the system.

In the early days of personal computers it was realised that there was a need for a number of standards which would apply to various elements of the computer system and the software and files these would contain. One of the most important of these is the way in which text files are created and presented - actually the characters that make up the text is what the standard applies to. Rather than develop a completely new system it was decided to adopt and modify an existing one, that which had been used for the transmission of messages across continental America on teletype machines, called ASCII.

ASCII is an acronym for American Standard Code for Information Interchange and it defines a series of unique codes for 128 characters, including Control Codes, numerals, alphabetical characters and punctuation marks. Each character is contained within a single BYTE, i.e. a string of 8 BITS or Binary Digits. The reason there were only 128 characters is because the character definition used only 7 of the 8 available bits, the final bit was used as a check digit. Thus, even though 8 bits will allow 255 characters, the use of the final digit for other purposes halved the total possible number of characters. At the time this was considered sufficient but within a very short period it was realised that additional characters were needed, e.g. foreign letters, graphics characters, etc. And this is where the fun began!

A Japanese company, Epson, developed a set of additional characters using the entire 8-bit word, the first 128 possible definitions were used for the standard ASCII set but they then used the remaining 127

ASCII files

possibles for a new set of characters. The additional characters are known as the Epson Extended ASCII Set and it is predominantly alphanumeric in nature. To this day most printers still use the Epson Extended ASCII characters. However, IBM, as the founding father of the personal computer, also developed an additional set. Again they removed the check digit and so were able to develop an additional 127 characters - unfortunately they created a different set to those used by Epson. This set is the IBM Extended ASCII Set and it is predominantly graphical in content.

The result is that there are two Extended Sets, the Epson one which occurs on printers and the IBM one which occurs on computers. (You can include any of the IBM Extended set in any file or document on the computer by pressing Alt and entering the three digit number for the character on the Numeric keypad, however you must use this one and not the normal number keys along the top of the main keyboard.) When you print the file, the extra characters will be converted to the Epson set and so the soft copy, i.e. what you can see on the screen, and the hard copy, i.e. what is printed, may well be very different. Some printers will allow you to emulate an IBM printer and so you can produce identical copies, but most emulate Epson and contain their Extended Character Set.

Allowable filenames

On any computer running under MS-DOS, you can define a filename using up to eight characters, plus an additional three for an extension. If you try to use more than eight then the extra is simply ignored. You should always try to name your files so that they are instantly recognisable - not just by you but by any other person who may have to use your computer.

For instance, you could decide to just number all your files, starting at 00000001 and progressing from there. As you create a new file you simply increase the number. In this way you could create a total of nearly ten million filenames. However, there are two major problems with using such a system.

1) You need to be able to remember which file is which. In fact you would probably have to keep a log of the file names and their contents in order to be able to use such a system. The trouble with this is that if you lose the log you will have real problems.

2) Under MS-DOS there is a limit to the number of files you can have on a disk. On a hard disk the maximum number of files you can have in the Root directory is 512. On a floppy disk the limit can be as low as 128. There is a way around the limit - use sub-directories - but even that does not answer the first problem.

The best way to name files is using alphabetical characters in such a way that the names reflect the file contents. Thus, if you write a letter to me, for example, you could call the file LETTERAB, LET-AB or ALANLET. Note that in each case you cannot use blank spaces - the filename must be continuous. Thus LET-AB, LET_AB, LETAB and LET'AB are all valid while LET AB is not. Similarly a full stop

Allowable filenames

is used to separate the filename from its extension. So, if you were to save the file as LET.AB when you then used **DIR** it would show, for example:

    LET   **AB**   1024   12-01-90   2:59a.m.

When you first acquire a computer or begin using one the eight characters seems a lot but as you create more and more files you begin to find that this is rather limiting and you have to become more creative in your choice and use of filenames. At the end of the day what you call your files is very much a matter of personal preferences, likes and dislikes. There is no right or wrong way - you can even use the numerical sequence mentioned above - simply use whichever is easiest for you. However, you should avoid giving any of your files the same name as program files as this may cause problems.

Reserved filenames

We have already mentioned that you can use up to eight characters for a filename and an additional three characters for the extension, although in neither case do you have to use the maximum number. You can call a file **A.1** or even **A** or more simply **1** if you wish, because you do not have to use an extension. However, you cannot use all the available characters for naming your files. For one thing MS-DOS makes no distinction between upper and lower case letters, thus A and a are identical as far as the operating system is concerned. This effectively limits your choice somewhat. The characters you can use are as follows:

A B C D E F G H I J K L M N O P Q R S T U V W X Y Z
0 1 2 3 4 5 6 7 8 9 ! £ % ^ & ( ) - _ { } ' @ # ~

all of which are accessible directly from the main keyboard. You can also use all of the Extended ASCII Character set. Hold down **Alt** and then type the number of the character on the Numeric keypad. As soon as you release the **Alt** key the character will appear. The extended set and their numbers are shown in the appendices. Any of these characters can be used within the eight letter filename or in the three character extension.

There are a number of words though that are reserved by MS-DOS for its own purposes and so you cannot use them for naming files, neither as a filename nor as an extension. You are not given any choice about this and you will find that you have to use something else. Certainly you should never use any of these reserved words as extensions because they will interfere with the way MS-DOS handles calls for commands.

The reserved words are:

39

Reserved filenames

AUX

Which is short for Auxiliary and it refers to the communications port into which you can connect a number of other devices, e.g. a modem.

BAS

Used as an extension by any program which is written in BASIC.

BAT

This is used as an extension for batch files.

COM

Refers to the communications serial port, it will usually have a number attached, e.g. COM1, and it is also used as the extension for certain programs.

CON

Short for Console and it refers to the keyboard and/or the monitor.

Reserved filenames

EXE

Used as an extension for executable files.

LPT

Refers to the line printer parallel ports.

PRN

Also refers to the printer

SYS

Reserved name for system files.

In addition to these words you also cannot use certain standard characters, either in the filename or the extension. These characters are the first 32 ASCII characters plus the following:

" $ * + = [ ] : ; | \ < , > . ? /
and a blank space.

As with the eight character filename you can use any of the acceptable characters for an extension. Again you do not have to use all three characters. By combining the filename and extension you can create more dynamic names for your files. This applies especially when you are creating sub-directories. In the normal course of events you

Reserved filenames

would create a sub-directory using only the first eight characters, but there is nothing to stop you using all eleven characters.

Because a directory is a special type of file you can include extensions when naming it. For example you may be using a spreadsheet and house it within its own directory, a habit well worth developing, and call it S'SHEET for example. Alternatively you could name the directory SPREADSH.EET, using the extension EET. This means when you do a directory listing you can see at a glance which directory contains what. However, some programs insist on their directories being given a specific name and this will be done as part of the installation routine. If this is the case then it is advisable not to change the name or you may find that the program does not operate correctly. The same criteria apply to ordinary filenames.

Disk terms

Throughout this book you will come across a number of terms and statements which are commonplace and generally used with impunity. Unfortunately they are rarely defined adequately and this can leave the new user groping around in the dark and having to guess at what is meant. In an effort to alleviate that problem I have decided to include a brief glossary of disk terms here.

Bit

The acronym for Binary Digit, i.e. it must be a 1 or 0, the smallest possible unit that the computer can work with. It tends to be used infrequently because people use the terms for numbers of bits instead.

Byte

Normally, a collection of eight Bits which is the minimum space required to define a single character. The byte forms the basis of all subsequent capacity measurement of both disks and the computer memory.

Disk

A contraction of Diskette hence the use of the letter k instead of a c. Even the Oxford English Dictionary uses this spelling. Computer disks are always referred to a 'disk' never as 'disc'.

Disk terms

Floppy Disk

A circular piece of non-woven polyester coated with a magnetisable material onto which data can be encoded. Floppy disks come in two main sizes, 3.5-inch, which are relatively new but becoming more common, and 5.25-inch, which are the old standard size. Then just to confuse everyone there are two capacities of each available. 3.5-inch disks can be 720 Kb (kilobytes) or 1.44 Mb (megabytes), while 5.25-inch disks can be 360 Kb or 1.2 Mb. Recently 3.5-inch 2.88 Mb floppies have become available though they are not in common use yet.

Formatting

The process of making the disk usable by the computer. During the formatting process the computer lays down a series of tracks and sectors on the disk surface. These then form the basis of the storage thereafter.

High Capacity Disks

A floppy disk which uses a high grade coating and thus allows data to be packed more precisely onto the disk. Such a disk also requires a special disk drive to be fitted to the machine. You should not use ordinary disks as high capacity ones or vice versa.

Disk terms

Kilobyte

A multiple defined as 1,024 bytes, usually written as 1 Kb, i.e. the space necessary to store 1024 characters. The reason that the multiple is 1024 and not 1000 is because it is a function of binary notation and 1 Kb is 2^{10} bytes.

Megabyte

A multiple defined as 1,024 Kb or 1,048,576 bytes, usually written as 1 Mb, which is used to denote the capacity of high density disks and hard disks. Again the definition is a function of binary notation and 1 Mb is 2^{20} bytes. 5.25-inch high density floppy disks have a capacity of 1.2 Mb while high density 3.5-inch disks have a capacity of 1.44 Mb. The difference is due to the number of sectors and tracks.

Sectors

Once the tracks have been laid down on the disk they are divided into arc shaped wedges - the sectors. It is the sector which forms the basis of disk storage. Different disks have a different number of sectors per track, the exact number depends on the capacity and size of the disk.

TPI

Acronym for Tracks Per Inch. 360 Kb 5.25-inch disks for example have 40, while 1.2 Mb 5.25-inch disks have 96.

Disk terms

Tracks

When a disk is formatted the computer lays down a series of circular tracks, one inside the other, on the disk. Note that the tracks are circular and not a spiral as on a record. Different numbers of tracks are laid down on the disks according to whether they are standard capacity, high density, 5.25-inch or 3.5-inch floppies. Hard disks are treated the same way but they have an enormously greater number of tracks than a floppy does.

Disk storage

The original IBM PC, as launched in 1980, used floppy disks as its main form of data storage and that custom continued for some time. Even today floppy disks still have a vital part to play in the transmission of data from one source to another. All software for example comes on floppy disks. The original standard was 5.25-inch 160 Kb disks but this was rapidly superseded by those having a capacity of 360 Kb. For a long time this was considered to be the standard disk within the PC market. They have now been superseded by larger capacities and new sizes. However, there are so many 360 Kb disks around that any change will have to be a slow and gradual process. Today there are two standard sized floppy disks. The older, which is gradually disappearing, is 5.25-inch 1.2 Mb and the newer is 3.5-inch 1.44 Mb. Then to confuse things there is a new 3.5-inch disk which has just appeared. This is 2.88 Mb, which provides a capacity of 2 Mb when formatted, but as yet they are still rare. MS-DOS 5.0 though does provide support for this new disk size.

All floppy disks are made from basically the same non-woven polyester material. This is coated with a resin which contains ultrafine ferrous particles in the case of low density disks, or microfine cobalt compounds in the case of high density disks. The material, which is actually in huge rolls, is then baked in a thermostatically controlled oven to bond the resin correctly to it. Once the rolls have been allowed to cool the actual disks are stamped out and then placed into their protective sleeves. In the case of 5.25-inch disks the sleeve is a flexible PVC material, usually coloured black, while 3.5-inch disks are enclosed in rigid PVC envelopes which provides much better protection. Standard density 3.5-inch disks, i.e. 720 Kb, normally have blue sleeves while high density ones have black covers. All quality disks these days are verified individually, i.e. checked to ensure that the coating is of sufficient quality to meet the manufacturer's standards.

Disk storage

In order to use the disk for data storage it must first be formatted, preferably in your own machine, but you can buy preformatted disks. This process, which is carried out by one of the MS-DOS external commands, lays down a series of rings called Tracks on the disk. These rings have no visible existence - they are simply patterns of magnetism. The number of tracks will depend on the type of disk being used and, more importantly, on the disk drive being used. You should only ever use the correct density disk in the corresponding drive. Never format a standard density disk in a high capacity drive or vice versa. If you do so then the disk will contain a large number of errors and its life will be shortened considerably. In addition, you cannot then reformat that disk in the proper drive because of the quality and pattern of tracks that it contains. A 360 Kb disk has 40 tracks laid down on it and they are 0.33 mm wide. 1.2 Mb disks have 80 tracks and they are 0.16 mm wide. Both types of 3.5-inch disk have 135 tracks and they are 0.115 mm wide. Note that the number of tracks expressed in the TPI figure is not actually used. In other words the used area of the disk is less than 1-inch wide!

Once the tracks are laid down the computer then divides these into sectors - arc shaped areas that form the basis of disk storage. Sectors are always 512 Bytes, regardless of the disk size or capacity. This is one of the very few true standards within the computer industry.

Hard disks on the other hand are made of aluminium coated with a magnetisable material. The actual discs are called Platters. These are stacked, one above the other, and fixed to a central core called a Spindle. The Read/Write Heads assembly is put into place and the whole thing is then enclosed in an airtight casing. When the hard disk is fitted to the computer it has to be connected, via ribbon cables, to a controller: that item of hardware which is responsible for actually operating the hard disk and accessing the data on it.

Disk storage

Unlike a floppy disk, a hard disk spins constantly while the computer has power. It usually rotates at, usually, 3,600 RPM (a floppy, on the other hand, spins at around 360 RPM) and it is easier to allow it to spin continuously rather than only on those occasions when you want to access it.

In many ways hard disks are very similar to floppy disks, i.e. they use the same method of formatting and assigning storage space, but they have three enormous advantages:

1) The access time, i.e. the length of time it takes them to find and present any file, is dramatically faster than a floppy. Typically, a hard disk can have an access time of around 18 milliseconds or less, depending on the coding system used, compared with four to six times that for a floppy disk. Floppy disks use a very old coding system which makes them very slow but extremely dependable.

2) A hard disk has a much greater capacity and thus removes the need to constantly switch disks as you run a program. Modern software tends to be on the large side, e.g. a typical word processor might need a total of 3 Mb to hold all of its files, and using it on a floppy based machine is a chore rather than a pleasure. The 'standard' size for a hard disk at the time of writing is around 70 Mb or 80 Mb, i.e. the equivalent of 200 standard 360 Kb floppy disks. However, this 'standard' hard disk continues to increase in capacity and by the end of the Nineties is likely to 1,200 Mb plus.

3) Dynamic storage abilities. A hard disk is much more than just a giant floppy disk. Using a hard disk is almost an art and you have to learn to use directories as an adjunct to your normal

Disk storage

usage. Using these you can 'tune' your storage requirements to a very high degree and so create a much more intensive method of storing data. In addition you can get into the realms of partitions, logical drives and physical drives, all of which make using a computer more rewarding.

The difference between using floppy storage and hard disk storage is best illustrated by an analogy. Using the former is the equivalent of cutting your lawn with a pair of scissors whereas using a hard disk machine is like doing the same thing with one of those mowers that you can sit on. In other words the hard disk makes your life so much easier and simpler it is well worth the trouble. It has to be said that using a hard disk wrongly can get you into a terrible mess awfully quickly. Nevertheless on the whole the advantages to using a hard disk far outweigh the disadvantages.

Physical and Logical

A physical drive is quite simply a drive you can see and/or touch and the phrase refers to the actual hardware. Note that the disk(s) are irrelevant - it is the drive unit itself which bears the nomenclature. Every computer, of necessity, has at least one floppy disk drive, whether this is a 5.25-inch or 3.5-inch makes no difference. Equally, this drive will always be Drive-A. This is the first physical drive.

At the front of the majority of computers there is usually a series of slots where the drives are housed. The number of slots depends on the total capacity of the carrier. The carrier is, generally, a moulded piece of plastic or metal into which the drives are secured. The carrier is sub-divided into lateral divisions which hold the drive units. Depending on the type of computer you have these drive slots will usually number between three and six, i.e. you can install that many drives. The slots which are currently vacant will normally have some form of sealing strip across them. This serves two purposes; one, it prevents dust and larger pieces of dirt from getting into the guts of the machine, and two, it gives an indication of how many additional drives you can add to that machine.

Fitting a new drive is relatively easy. Just follow the instructions which accompany the unit and you should have no problems. One thing that you may need to get, though, is a cable splitter. Every drive unit must have power and this is provided by a set of four thin cables with a connector at the free end, the other end of which goes into the power supply.

Unfortunately many computers provide only two or three power lines and if you already have that many drives fitted you will not have a free power line to connect to the new drive. The answer is to get a cable splitter. This is simply a connector with two sets of power lines running from it. You take one of the power lines from the power

Physical and Logical

supply, connect it into the main connector on the splitter and then you have two free ends to connect to the drives. Most dealers will be able to supply a cable splitter and generally they will make it up to any size you want.

A floppy disk drive is always a physical drive, i.e. it cannot be subdivided into other logical drives. It is only hard disks, and occasionally CD-ROM drives, which are partitioned into separate logical drives. Today most hard disk drives are half-height, which means that they occupy the same amount of space, in the carrier, that a floppy drive does. The advantage of this is that all drive units are now a standard size and so they can be interchanged easily and quickly.

When MS-DOS was originally created the standard amount of memory, i.e. RAM, was 64 Kb. Hard disk drives did not exist, except for mainframe computers and these were huge and so not applicable to the new desktop machines. The result was that the original release of MS-DOS, i.e. Version 1.0, did not have the ability to communicate with and control hard disks. It was based primarily on tape drives, using cassette tapes as the main storage medium. Very quickly it was found that such storage, known as serial storage because the data is written or read in a linear sequence, was too slow for the new PC and so Microsoft upgraded the operating system to handle floppy disks.

For a number of years this was all that MS-DOS could handle and it was, apparently, sufficient. But then Shugart Associates created the first hard disk for the PC. By today's standards it was very small, 5 Mb was the maximum size available, but the advent of the drive meant that MS-DOS had to be upgraded again. Microsoft took the opportunity to rewrite major chunks of the operating system at the same time and the new version was 2.0. This allowed for control of hard disk drives but it imposed a maximum limit on the size they

Physical and Logical

could be - 32 Mb. At the time this seemed to be a huge amount, after all it was six times the size of the drives currently available, and so everyone was happy.

But then, as generally happens, the technology involved in hard disks improved and the size of the drives available began to increase at a phenomenal rate. 10 Mb drives, then 20, 30, 40 and beyond appeared and were used. The 32 Mb limit that MS-DOS imposed became an obstacle to using the hard disk efficiently. A number of computer manufacturers got round the problem by tweaking MS-DOS in various ways but this was less than satisfactory. Eventually Microsoft upgraded MS-DOS dramatically, with Version 4.0, which removed the 32 Mb limit - but it had problems and versions of MS-DOS less than 4.0 are still used on the majority of computers.

So how do you get around the problem if you are using MS-DOS 3.2 or 3.3 and you have a 70 Mb drive? Quite simply you partition it into chunks of 32 Mb or less. Each partition then becomes a separate logical drive and is accordingly assigned its own drive designator letter. Thus if you have a 70 Mb drive you would have to divide it into three logical drives and then you would then have Drive-C, which is always the first partition, Drive-D and Drive-E - but they are all part of the same physical drive. The MS-DOS program that allows you to do this is FDISK, which we will cover in detail later.

MS-DOS 4.0 removed the need to partition a drive in this way, but a case can still be made for such sub-division; however, it now becomes a matter of personal choice rather than necessity. For instance, you could decide to place all your textual programs, e.g. word processor, text editor, etc., onto one logical drive, have all your graphic applications on another, and have all your accounts on a third. This would then allow you to categorise your programs and

Physical and Logical

data files and ensure that they are all kept separate. Essentially what MS-DOS 4.0 does is allow you freedom of choice, as regards disk storage, for the first time.

MS-DOS 5.0 does impose a limit on how large a single partition can be but as this is 1 Gb plus it hardly concerns us for the moment - though it may do by the end of the decade. The net result for the moment is that you can have a partition of whatever size you want.

Directories

Using partitions to separate your program types is all well and good but, generally speaking, the computer and its associated disk storage works most efficiently if the partitions are the maximum size possible. This effectively means, if you are running any version of MS-DOS earlier than Version 4.0, that you want the partitions to be as close to the 32 Mb limit as it is possible to get. Thus, if your machine is fitted with a 32 Mb drive you will be using a single logical drive. So how do you sub-divide this to allow the separation of your programs into types? The answer is to use directories. Many people, especially those who are new to computers, get confused about directories - generally because they have not been explained properly.

On every disk there is, as far as MS-DOS is concerned, always one directory - the Root. This directory is the entire capacity of the disk. When you place a newly formatted floppy into Drive-A and enter **DIR** you will get a listing like this:

Volume in drive A is untitled
Directory of A:

File not found

The first line gives you the name, if any, that has been given to the disk using the Label command which can be part of the Format command. The second line tells you where on the disk you are looking. The A:\, in particular the backslash character, tells you that you are in the Root Directory. The last line says that there are no files on the disk - because, in this case, it has been newly formatted.

You will get the same message if you have wiped all the files from an older disk. Unfortunately, because of the way that the MS-DOS DIR command works, you cannot tell how much space there is on the

Directories

blank disk. To find out you can use another MS-DOS command - **CHKDSK** which is short for Check Disk and it gives you much more information:

          Volume FLOPPY DISK created 28 Feb 1990 7:09p

              1213952 bytes total disk space
                    0 bytes in 1 hidden files
              1213952 bytes available on disk

               655360 bytes total memory
               530448 bytes free

This time the first line tells you the name that has been applied to the disk, but it also tells you the date and time when the disk was formatted. Then it tells you how much space there should be on the disk. Note that it gives the maximum possible space and not the actual space. The third line informs you of how much space has been consumed with hidden files, e.g. the MS-DOS system files, and in this case there are no such files. The following line then tells you the total capacity of the disk that is available for storing files.

If the disk was damaged in any way there would also be another line that tells you how much space on the disk was lost due to bad sectors, i.e. areas of the disk where the magnetic coating was damaged and so could not be used for storing data. Any such damaged sectors will reduce the total amount of disk space available.

The first of the bottom two lines tell you how large the RAM is - this can never exceed 655,360 bytes when running under MS-DOS. The final line says how much of that memory is available for running programs. (In this case the amount was reduced to 530,448 bytes

Directories

because of memory resident programs.) Normally however you would not use CHKDSK except on those occasions when you want to validate a suspect disk. We will cover the command in detail later.

Going back to **DIR**, if the disk contains files you will get a listing like this:

Volume in drive A is unlabelled
Directory of A:

FILENAME 001	6 28-02-90 11:22a
FILENAME 002	37 28-02-90 11:23a
FILENAME 003	67 28-02-90 11:24a
FILENAME 004	127 28-02-90 11:24a

4 File(s)   1210880 bytes free

This gives the disk label again, the current area of the disk you are logged onto, i.e. the Root, and a listing of all the files it contains, plus their sizes and times of creation.

The Root Directory of any disk can only contain so many files, in the case of the high density disk we have been using as an example it is 512 files - the same limit applies to hard disks by the way. Thus, even if all the files were the size of FILENAME.001 in the example above, you could only store 512 of them on the disk - even though their total size would be only 3072 bytes. Don't forget that each file occupies one Cluster, the minimum amount of space required, and so the total area the files would be occupying is 256 Kb in the case of this high density disk, i.e. 512 bytes per Cluster. Even though you would then have nearly 1 Mb of unused space you cannot place any more files on the disk. MS-DOS imposes this limit and there is, apparently, nothing you can do about it.

Directories

Well, there is - you can use directories. A directory is a special kind of file into which you can store other files as separate entities. Think of the disk as a filing cabinet, the whole cabinet represents the total capacity of the disk, i.e. 1.2 Mb in this case. Each file is a distinct piece of paper which contains data. You can put the pieces of paper into the filing cabinet any way you wish but it makes much more sense to file them in some kind of order. The cardboard sleeves within the drawers represent the directories. Each one is used to store related pieces of paper but even so the sheets are still separate and distinct.

Normally you would not use directories on a 360 Kb or 720 Kb disk (although there is no reason why you shouldn't if you wish) because you will run out of Clusters to use long before you reach the 512 file limit. But once you start using high density disks and hard disks they become essential. Within any directory, other than the Root Directory, you can store an unlimited number of files - subject only to the total disk capacity. Because each directory is a file, albeit a special one, the directory itself occupies disk space - usually a single Cluster - but within this you can then store all the files you need to. You can even place directories within directories within directories. MS-DOS will not allow you to have more than nine levels of directories, the Root Directory being the first level. Generally speaking you will not want to have more than three or four levels though, otherwise the structure you create becomes unwieldy and cumbersome.

Directories can be extremely useful and their main function is to allow you to manage your files and disk storage effectively. You can create a directory without any thought, just add new directories as you need them. The trouble with doing this is that the structure soon becomes unstable and it takes you a long time to move from one directory to another. Much better to plan the structure first and then set it in place so that you have a solid foundation.

Directory Structure

To create the basic structure you need first to know what programs and associated files you want to have on your disk, and a rough idea of how they are to be organised. Ideally you want to keep the Root Directory as empty of files as possible; it should contain only the three system files, two of which are hidden, the CONFIG.SYS, and the AUTOEXEC.BAT. Everything else should be in directories. One point which should be borne in mind is that a heavily layered directory structure is cumbersome and unwieldy. For preference you should not have more than three layers, including the Root, although this may not be possible.

There are no hard and fast rules about a directory structure - simply some points to bear in mind.

- A simple structure is easier to maintain and move around. If you make it complex and multi-layered then you will spend a lot of time moving through it to find the files you want.

- Always place associated files together in the same directory. That way you can quickly find any given file instead of losing time looking for it. Remember what the directories are for - they make disk and file management easier.

- Give directories simple, explanatory names. Many of today's software packages come complete with an installation routine, though some are better than others, and you will find they tend to create directories relating to the program. For instance Windows uses Windows, PageMaker uses PM, Deluxe Paint II uses DPAINT2, and so on. You should adopt the same approach and name directories so you will instantly know what they are.

Directory Structure

- Plan the structure - don't just create it without forethought. A deliberate structure has a certain elegance and finesse to it, an indiscriminate one looks untidy and needlessly shoddy.

- Always make a spare directory, one that can be used for copying files that you may want but are unsure about. For instance I call the one I use JUNK. If you have such a directory then you can copy the files to this, while you pick and choose which ones you actually want and then move them to their final home. The unwanted files can then be deleted quickly and easily. Never copy files into the Root Directory other than in exceptional circumstances.

Keeping these points in mind you can begin to plan and finally create your directory structure. Do it on paper first and only when you are satisfied should you build it on the computer.

Because directories are special kinds of files they have to be manipulated with their own commands, of which there are three. The first, MKDIR or MD, either being an abbreviation for Make Directory, is used to create the directory using the syntax **MD [**DRIVE**]\ [**PATH**]\[**DIRECTORY**]**. If the drive and path are omitted then the directory will be created as a sub-directory of the one you are currently logged onto. A directory name can be eleven characters long, eight as the main name and three as an extension, although it is common practise not to use more than eight - thus directories can be easily distinguished from filenames when listed using **DIR/W**. As with filenames you cannot use any of the reserved or forbidden characters or words.

It is possible to create directories at a distance by including the full path. For example, if you are logged onto Drive-C and you wish to create a directory on Drive-D, simply enter **MD D:\[**DIRECTORY**]**. You

Directory Structure

can create sub-directories in the same way: **MD D:\[DIRECTORY]\[SUB-DIRECTORY]** providing that the first level directory exists. Notice that you must include the backslash between the drive designator and the first directory and then between the first directory and the sub-directory.

The only error message you are likely to get using the command is **Unable to create directory**. This occurs if you try to use any of the forbidden characters or words or if you are trying to use the same name twice. You can only have one directory of any given name in any other directory. For example, suppose you had a directory called ALPHA in the Root. You cannot then have another directory of the same name at that level. However if you go down one level, even into ALPHA itself, and then input **MD ALPHA** you will have no problem.

To delete a directory you must use the command RMDIR, RD for short, the abbreviation for Remove Directory. If you were to use **DEL [DIRECTORY]** then you would delete every file contained in that directory except those which are Read-Only. This is a useful way of removing all the files but it does not remove the directory. The syntax for the command is **RD [DRIVE]\[PATH]\[DIRECTORY]**. As with MD you can use the command at a distance to remove directories on other drives.

If, when you use the command, you get an error message saying **Invalid path, not directory, or directory not empty** it simply means what it says - one of the few examples where the error message is helpful! Either you have input the path incorrectly, misspelling it perhaps, the directory name is wrong or the directory still contains files. You cannot remove a directory that is not empty. You can check the first two possible causes by pressing **F3** - this will

Directory Structure

display the last keyboard input again so you can check the spelling. If that is correct then the last cause is the only remaining culprit. Enter **DEL [DIRECTORY]** to delete all the files and then try **RD [DIRECTORY]** again. If it still does not work then you must move into the directory itself and physically check for the presence of files by using DIR. If there are no files visibly present then the most likely problem is that there are Hidden files. You can only get at these with a utility program, such as Norton or PC Tools.

To move around the directory structure you use the final special command, CHDIR or CD for short. This is an abbreviation for Change Directory and it allows you to do just that. The syntax is **CD [PATH]\[DIRECTORY]** - note no drive specifier. You cannot change to another drive and directory in one operation. If while on C: you input **CD D:\[DIRECTORY]** then nothing apparently happens. However, if you then enter **D:** you will find that you are in the directory mentioned in the previous command. Normally though you would change drive and then change directory.

The command syntax will also affect how it works.

- **CD [DIRECTORY]** allows you to move into a sub-directory of the current directory. For example, you can move from the root down into Alpha by entering **CD ALPHA**.

- **CD** will take you directly back to the Root Directory of the current drive, e.g. from within Alpha if you enter **CD** you will go back to the root.

- **CD\[DIRECTORY]** allows you to move directly to another directory off the Root - you must obviously know the name of the target directory. For example you can move directly from Alpha to

Directory Structure

Beta by entering **CD\BETA** which takes you from Alpha up to the root and then down into Beta.

- **CD..** simply takes you back up one level, i.e. to the parent of the current directory. From either Alpha or Beta this command will take you back to the root.

- **CD..\[DIRECTORY]** takes you back up one level and down to the named directory which is on the same level as the current directory. In certain circumstances they can refer to the Root but it is more normal to allude to the Root using the backslash. A single dot, which is displayed when using the **DIR** command, signifies the current directory.

Disk areas

Whenever you format a disk, regardless of its type, MS-DOS immediately grabs a certain amount of the available capacity for its own use. It does not matter whether the disk contains the system files or not but it will always contain the following areas. Without these the disk is unusable by MS-DOS.

Firstly there is the Boot Sector. This contains the basic information about the disk, i.e. the information about the number of bytes per sector, the number of sectors per track, the number of sectors per cluster and so on. If the Boot Sector is damaged, for whatever reason, then the entire disk becomes unusable, for obvious reasons. In such a circumstance the only recourse normally available to you is to reformat the disk, which will wipe out any data that the disk contains in the process. However, if you are using a hard disk this can be disastrous and so you should have a set of utility programs, like Norton Utilities, which can be used to repair the damage.

Secondly, there is the File Allocation Table - FAT for short. The FAT consists of a table of entries which gives MS-DOS details of the locations of the files that the disk contains. (In fact there are actually two sets of the FAT and MS-DOS needs both of them to use the disk properly.) The file locations are recorded by giving the starting cluster of a file and the number of clusters that the file occupies. If the FAT is damaged you may be unable to access the file concerned, although this rarely happens because MS-DOS simply cross checks with the other copy of the table. However if the FAT does become damaged or corrupted, you generally have to reformat the disk again and thus lose any data it contains in the process.

Disk areas

Thirdly, there is the Root Directory. As well as being used to hold files this also contains descriptive details of the files and the volume label of the disk. If you want the disk to be bootable then the first two files on the disk must be the system files, if they are located anywhere else then the computer cannot boot from that disk. This is why if you want to create a bootable disk you would normally format it and copy the system files at the same time.

The size of the missing capacity depends on the type of disk you are using, for instance on a 360 Kb disk the Boot, FAT and Root occupy 6 Kb and so reduce the total capacity to 354 Kb.

Part Three

Resources

Hardware

When someone mentions the word Computer, what do you see in your mind's eye? A small, semi-cubical box with a thing like a portable TV on top and a keyboard attached by a coiled cable, perhaps? Or a tall, thin, tower structure with the TV beside it, or just a TV screen and a keyboard? It is likely that whatever your mental picture of the computer it only contains the external visible components of the system. Well, you don't see a load of transistors, chips, wires and what have you, do you?

A computer, regardless of its external appearance, is a machine made up of separate elements which all interact together to make a viable system for dealing with data. The external bits and pieces are what you see and what most people consider to be the whole, but there is slightly more to it than that. What follows is a brief rundown of what the computer can contain. It is not meant to be definitive - it merely covers the most salient features.

The main part of the system as far as the user is concerned is the bit you look at - the monitor. Monitors come in all shapes and sizes but the most common sizes are 12-inch and 14-inch - measured across the diagonal of the screen as with televisions. As well as their size and shape there is also the type of monitor. This determines the quality of resolution, i.e. the clarity of the display. There are a number of standards for monitors which determine how good the clarity, resolution and display should be, each one is usually designated by an acronym - except for the first.

Hercules

This is a very old standard and has been around almost as long as the original IBM PC. It is normally used as text only and it

Hardware

allows you to display 40 or 80 columns, i.e. characters across the screen, by 25 lines. With a resolution of 720 pixels by 350 pixels (A pixel being the smallest point on the screen which can be independently lit.) Hercules monitors have the best resolution and the clearest characters of all monitors. Most people are surprised to learn that a Hercules monitor will display graphics but it can. There is a drawback however: because it is monochrome all the colours are displayed as greyscales, i.e. various densities of grey. Unfortunately some of today's most common commercial software packages will not run on Hercules monitors because they are dependent on using colour monitors - although such programs are numerically few.

CGA

Short for Colour Graphics Adaptor. This is the lowest quality colour monitor you can buy - although they are now becoming very rare, thankfully, and the only place you will find them is on very cheap, low quality machines. It can display the same number of lines and characters as the Hercules but the quality of the display is very much poorer. The CGA monitor can display colour graphics at a resolution of 320 pixels by 200 but is limited to four, very poor, colours. It can also be used in monochrome mode, i.e. using greyscales, which increases the resolution to 640 by 200 pixels.

Hardware

EGA

Enhanced Graphics Adaptor. This will display the same number of lines and characters as the previous two and these are nearly as good as those on a Hercules monitor. When it comes to colours EGA monitors will allow you to display different ranges, from 16 colours at a resolution of 640 by 350 pixels down to 320 by 200 pixels using only 4 colours. Running the monitor in monochrome mode will allow you a resolution of 720 by 350 pixels and 16 greyscales. As with CGA these are becoming rare although there are still a large number of machines around that use EGA.

VGA

Short for Video Graphics Array. This is the monitor type that became the standard fitted to the majority of AT's and higher priced PC's that were supplied in the last couple of years of the previous decade. The VGA monitor emulates all the previous types but with a clarity, in full colour, that more than matches Hercules. The standard VGA resolution is 640 by 480 pixels using up to 16 colours but it can be switched to produce a resolution of 320 by 200 pixels and use up to 64 colours at once. In monochrome mode it is limited to 64 greyscales.

Super VGA

This is the de facto standard today. It is capable of displaying all the previous resolutions plus a much higher definition. The standard for SVGA can be anything up to 1024 by 780 pixels

Hardware

displaying up to 256 colours but then everything appears minute. Better, perhaps, is the 640 by 480 using 256 colours which can provide very dynamic displays.

There are other monitor types available but they tend to available as an extra, i.e. they are not normally fitted as standard, and they also tend to be rather expensive. However, a word of caution, there is a great deal of difference between monitors from different manufacturers. In addition you must have the correct adaptor card fitted to your machine in order to use the monitor.

Keyboards

Nowadays there are two standards for keyboards. The first is the one fitted to the early PC's. It generally had 86 or 88 keys and the function keys are arranged in two lines down the left hand side of the main keypad. You will find this keyboard fitted to the majority of those machines that use an 8088 or 8086 microchip. The second standard is the AT keyboard. This normally has 101 or 102 keys. The function keys are arranged in a line above the main keypad and it also has an extra set of cursor movement keys, independent of those on the numeric keypad.

System Boxes

Finally there is the system box itself. Until very recently there was only one kind of system box - the Desktop. This is a big, chunky box with the disk drive(s) in the front and the monitor normally sits on top of it. Latterly, however, new shapes have

Hardware

appeared - the tower and mini-tower. These are essentially a desktop turned on its side. Mini-towers are about the same size and stand on the desk, full towers sit on the floor under the desk. The major advantage of full towers is that the system box tends to be bigger, so you can get more into it, but because it is tall and slim you can stand it at the side of a desk and just have the monitor taking up desk space. There are also portable computers, laptops, hand held and even pen operated computers. There are almost as many different designs for these as there are manufacturers!

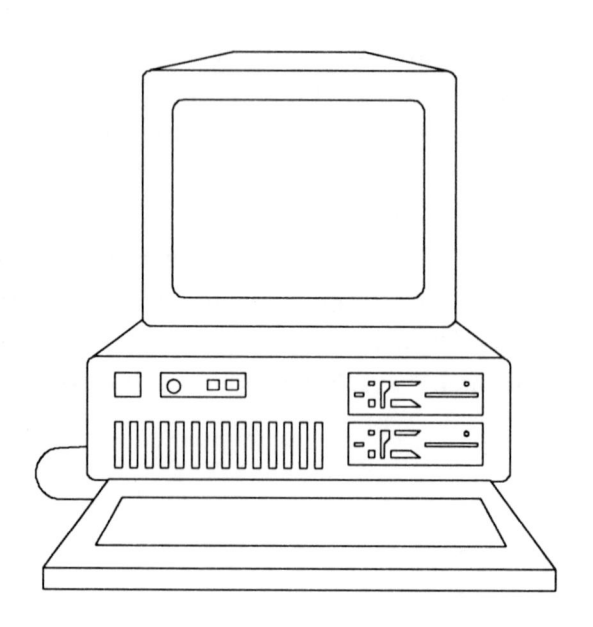

Chips

At the heart of every PC or AT is a microchip - the engine that drives the computer. The chip makes an enormous difference to the speed of the machine when it comes to handling calculations. It also makes a difference to how fast the data can be accessed, but not as much as you might think. What actually controls disk access speed is the controller for the disk drive, although the address bus of the chip, that part of it that accepts data from the drive via the controller, does make a slight difference.

The IBM PC and compatibles, including the AT's, are built around the 8000 Series microchip developed by the Intel Corporation. Because each chip in the 8000 series is compatible with all the preceding chips it means that any new chip can run all the existing software base that has been developed for previous chips within the same series. The series includes:

8086

This is the first chip in the series and it was developed by Intel in 1976. It possesses a 16-bit data bus and can address up to 1 Mb of RAM using a 20-bit address bus. Used mainly in low cost, minimum configuration machines. There are probably more 8086 based computers in existence than anything else because the chip is used for things like cash machines and tills in supermarkets.

8088

This is really a cut-down version of the 8086 and it was introduced in 1978. IBM used this chip as the base of the

Chips

original PC, rather than the 8086 because it was cheaper and they thought that people would be disinclined to buy the more powerful and faster 8086. The 8088 has the same internal architecture as the 8086 but it has only an 8-bit data bus. This means that it is much slower in accessing data from disk or memory. Again though it can address up to 1 Mb of RAM using a 20-bit address bus.

Apart from the differences in the data bus size there is no real difference between the 8088 and the 8086, in fact the chips are identical internally. However, the larger bus on the 8086 means that it does tend to run slightly faster because it can read and write the data quicker. The original PC used an 8088 running at 4.77 MHz, i.e. it could perform just under 5 million operations per second, and this speed is used as the base measure against which all other chips are matched. It is still possible to purchase 8088 chips, they are very cheap and so they allow the construction of very basic, low level and low price machines. However, the technology of the rest of the peripheral devices used in today's computers means that the 8088, or the 8086, actually acts as a brake on the speed with which the computer can operate.

80186

This was introduced in 1982 and it is really just an enhanced version of the 8086. It has a 16-bit data bus and can address 1 Mb of RAM using a 20-bit address bus. However, it was not taken up by the computer industry as a whole and although a few machines based on the 80186 were developed they soon faded away. Nowadays the 80186 is making a come-back as an

Chips

embedded controller on EISA and MCA add-on cards, i.e. cards that control other devices within the machine.

80286

Launched in 1981, this chip is special in a number of ways. It has a 16-bit data bus, can address up to 16 Mb of RAM using a 24-bit address bus, and it has a built in real time clock. It is fully compatible with the earlier chips in the series and so any software written for the 8088 or the 8086 will run on an 80286. In order to do so the 80286 operates in two different modes - Real, which is identical to the 8086 and 8088, and Protected, which is specific to the 80286. (In reality the 80286 is used as a fast 8086 and nobody really bothers with the multitasking ability - for one thing, you cannot switch between modes without rebooting the machine.) Running in Real Mode the chip can return a very impressive performance. Typically the 80286 will operate at two and a half times the speed of an 8086 when running identical software at the same clock speed, or 12 times faster than the original PC. (Curiously enough it can also run faster than a 25 MHz 80386 or produce speeds comparable with a 25 MHz 80486!) The fastest 80286 available from Intel is 12 MHz, although other chip manufacturers do provide faster versions.

80386

If the 80286 was a major step forward then the 80386 was a giant leap. A full 32-bit chip, it uses a 32-bit data bus, is capable of addressing a massive 4,096 Mb of RAM using a 32-bit

Chips

address bus and is capable of true multitasking. Launched in 1985, it was not commercially available in a computer until late 1986. Like the 80286 it can operate in Real or Protected Mode, however it can also use a third mode - Virtual Real.

The major difference between the 80286 and the 80386 is that the latter can multitask correctly. Further, it can switch from one mode to the other without having to be rebooted. One major fault lies in its compatibility with the rest of the 8000 series. As a result of this the chip cannot run standard MS-DOS software in Real mode any faster than an 80286 can - in fact sometimes it will be slower than its earlier cousin!

80386SX

Because initially the 80386 was so expensive, (although it is much less so now due to market forces) and also because it had capabilities which could not be fully utilised, Intel produced a cut down version of the chip, the 80386SX. This chip bears the same relationship to the 80386 as the 8088 does to the 8086 - i.e. it has much of the same internal architecture but its links with the rest of the machine are limited. The 80386SX has a 16-bit data bus, making data handling slower, and a 24-bit address bus which limits its maximum RAM usage to 16 Mb. However, internally it can produce the same processing speeds as the 80386. Due to its low price, machines based around this chip are fast becoming the entry level systems and are displacing the 80286 machines.

Chips

80486

This chip runs 40% faster than the 80386 at the same clock speed with the result that a 25 MHz 80486 is faster than a 33 MHz 80386. In addition it has a built in co-processor. Prior to this chip if you wanted to do a large amount of number crunching you had to purchase and fit a co-processor chip, designated by a 7 rather than a 6 at the end of the chip number, e.g. 80287 or 80387. However the 80486 has the co-processor already on board and so there is no need to fit additional chips. Intel recently announced a 50 MHz 80486.

80486SX

This is brand new and has only just been released. Basically it is a cut down 80486 and lacks the co-processor. Whether or not they are taken up in quantity by the industry is questionable and only time will tell.

Booting up

When you turn the computer on, a process called booting up, the machine performs a number of functions - none of which you normally see. The first thing it does is run the Power On Self Test. The POST is a series of tests which check the major components of the system including the CPU, i.e. the main chip; the ROM and the RAM; the motherboard circuitry; and all the major peripherals such as controller cards and disk drives. None of the tests is very extensive, they are intended only to find gross errors and it is possible for a computer to pass its POST but still fail to function. Generally speaking, any errors found during the POST will produce one of two kinds of error message, a visual one or an audio one.

One of the first things you should notice when booting up any computer is a beep. This is simply to inform you that the power has been turned on. If this does not occur then there is likely to be a fault with the power supply. A continuous beep or a series of short beeps also indicates power supply problems. Normally the manual that accompanies your machine will give details of the errors and how they are presented during the POST. The main visual message you will see is the memory test results. Normally every PC or AT will display the maximum amount of RAM that is present as it is checked. But this only refers to on-board RAM, any expanded memory will not be checked as part of the POST, although it will normally have it own diagnostic checks.

Having completed the POST the computer will then load the operating system - provided it can find it. The most frequent error that can occur at this point is caused by someone leaving a disk in one of the floppy drives. As the disk will not normally contain the system files the computer responds with an error message telling you so. Don't panic - just remove the disk and press any key. The computer then continues to look for the operating system elsewhere.

Booting up

Once the main operating system files have been loaded MS-DOS takes over. It looks for and implements the CONFIG.SYS file and its contents, setting up any devices that may be necessary, and then it looks for and loads the AUTOEXEC.BAT. Note however, that you do not have to have either of these in order for the computer to operate - it can function without them. However if they are not present you cannot tailor the system to your own desires. Once all the files have been loaded you will normally be presented with a blank screen except for the system prompt in the top left hand corner, e.g. C>_ - this simply tells you that the computer is ready and waiting for your instructions.

The system prompt is not, as many people think, the letter and flashing cursor that appears at the top of the screen - or at least not entirely. The characters you see at the top of the screen are actually in two parts. The first is the drive designator, i.e. the C, and its function is simply to tell you what logical drive you are currently logged onto. To change to another drive simply enter the drive letter followed by a colon, e.g. A: or F: or W:, and the system will transport you there.

You can customise the prompt in a vast range of different ways - in fact the prompt is probably the one part of the system you can adapt more than any other. Normally you would set the prompt in your AUTOEXEC.BAT but you can change it at any time directly from the keyboard, provided you are not within an application program, because the command which does this is an MS-DOS internal one.

Probably the best cursor you can have is the one that tells you not only which drive you are logged onto but also where you are within the directory structure. To get this enter PROMPT PG. Each pair of characters, e.g. $P, has a specific function and they must be used

79

Booting up

in pairs. In this case $P is the part that yields the position on the directory structure. The $G merely produces a greater than sign, i.e. >. Note you do not have to change the part that tells you what drive you are on, because that is automatic.

While **PG** is the most useful prompt you can have, you are not limited to using the command this way: you can create a much more exotic prompt. For instance suppose that you wanted to know the Time, Date, Drive and Directory, all on separate lines and then you wanted anything you typed to appear below this but separated by a blank line. To achieve this you would use **PROMPT T_D_P_$_**. As soon as you enter this you get a prompt that looks something like this:

> **12:45:01.23**
> **Fri 30-03-1990**
> **C:**

As far as MS-DOS is concerned anything you enter on the keyboard, while you are not within an application program, is a command and it is treated as such. Suppose that you enter your name. MS-DOS looks through all the files in the current directory to see if what you have entered matches a COM, EXE or BAT file in that directory. It always follows a very strict hierarchical order in this search.

First it looks to find a match with those files that have an extension of COM. Then it looks for a match for a file having an EXE extension, and finally it checks those with BAT. It ignores all other files. If what you have input matches an existing file then MS-DOS will execute that program. If there is no match you will get a message saying **Bad Command or Filename**.

Booting up

If you have set a PATH, MS-DOS looks first in the current directory and then it searches each directory mentioned on the path in the order they are given. Assume that your PATH had four directories mentioned, ALPHA, BETA, GAMMA and DELTA, and you were logged onto a fifth directory called EPSILON. When you enter your name MS-DOS checks through EPSILON to find a match with those files having a COM extension. Then it checks ALPHA, then BETA, then GAMMA and finally DELTA - still searching for a COM extension. When it doesn't find a match it comes back to EPSILON and begins checking for a file with an .EXE extension. It then checks all the directories again trying to find a corresponding file with an .EXE extension. Finally it comes back to EPSILON again and looks for the name with an extension of .BAT before going off and checking all the directories again trying to find a batch file with that name. Only when it has exhausted all these possibilities will it give you the error message saying Bad Command or Filename.

There are two points to note about this. Firstly, MS-DOS ignores any full stop and anything that follows it in the input. Secondly, the search is hierarchical. This means that if you have three files, all named LEMUR but the first is a COM file, the second an EXE file and the third a batch file, then MS-DOS would never find the last two. Every time it searches for the filename it will find LEMUR.COM, execute that and therefore stop searching. Even if you enter LEMUR.BAT, MS-DOS will still not find the file you want because it ignores the full stop and the BAT extension, instead it finds and executes LEMUR.COM. So the moral of the story is - be careful about the filenames you assign to your files.

Internal or External

We have already mentioned how MS-DOS searches for a match to your input, but there is a little more to it than that. The operating system comes complete with a range of commands that are built-in, i.e. they become operable every time you boot up the computer. These commands are called Internal Commands. The advantage of these is that they do not exist as separate programs which have to be stored on the disk before MS-DOS can use them. Because they are part of the operating system they are always available for use.

The reason they exist is due to the fact that when MS-DOS was first created, the programmers concerned decided on what commands the user, i.e. you, would need. What they ended up with was a rather long list and if they had built them all into the system it would not have fitted into the memory available on the early machines. So they split the list into two unequal modules. One part contains all those commands that are necessary but which are not likely to be used on a regular basis. These are the External Commands. They exist as separate programs that have to be stored on a disk and accessed as a normal program would be.

The second part was what the programmers considered MS-DOS must have, i.e. the commands which would be used most often and which therefore it made sense to include within the operating system itself. These are the Internal Commands. They include a range of specific commands as well as those that are normally used exclusively within batch files. It has to be said that they are a curious mixture, because some can be used directly, i.e. straight from the keyboard, but others can't. Some of them are almost redundant. The Internal Commands are:

Internal or External

BREAK	CALL	CHDIR
CLS	COPY	CTTY
DATE	DEL	DIR
ECHO	ERASE	ERRORLEVEL
EXIT	FOR	GOTO
IF	MKDIR	NOT
PATH	PAUSE	PROMPT
REM	REN	SET
SHIFT	TIME	TYPE
VER	VERIFY	VOL

The External Commands are:

APPEND	ASSIGN	ATTRIB
BACKUP	CHKDSK	COMMAND
COMP	DEBUG	DISKCOMP
DISKCOPY	EDLIN	EXE2BIN
FASTOPEN	FC	FDISK
FIND	FORMAT	GRAFTABL
GRAPHICS	JOIN	KEYB
LABEL	LINK	MEM
MODE	MORE	NLSFUNC
PRINT	RECOVER	REPLACE
RESTORE	SELECT	SHARE
SORT	SUBST	SYS
TREE	XCOPY	

Devices

Devices are those parts of the computer system which are not included as part of the motherboard configuration. In other words they are peripheral devices which need to be installed separately in order for them to work. A device does not have to be hardware though, it can be software as in the case of ANSI.SYS which simply controls the monitor and how it works. To use a device you must load the appropriate driver for it. Drivers are programs which let the operating system recognise the devices, e.g. a modem, printer, or a mouse. Some drivers are already installed with MS-DOS. Others, called installable device drivers, can be installed as and if you need them. Drivers include:

ANSI.SYS

Allows you to use ANSI escape sequences in real mode. An ANSI escape sequence is a series of characters developed by the American National Standards Institute and they are designed to produce particular effects on the monitor. Specifically, you can change graphics functions and affect the movement of the cursor. Modern day software rarely needs ANSI.SYS but some older software, and especially Shareware, tends to be dependent on it being installed. If you load a program and all you get is meaningless drivel then the program probably needs to have ANSI.SYS loaded to work correctly.

COUNTRY.SYS

Configures the machine to country specific details, e.g. the format for the date and time.

Devices

DISPLAY.SYS

Used to control the monitor.

DRIVER.SYS

Allows you to use external disk drives rather than just those which have been installed into the carrier and hence are part of the machine.

EMM386.EXE

Allows MS-DOS programs on 80386 and 80486 systems to emulate expanded memory in extended memory. The driver supports the Lotus, Intel, and Microsoft (LIM) Expanded Memory Specification (EMS) 4.0. It also allows you to use memory more effectively and allocate it better.

HIMEM.SYS

Allows MS-DOS programs on 80286 or better systems with extended memory to access the extended memory independent of machine configuration. It also allows MS-DOS programs to use an extra 64 Kb region of memory for code and data. HIMEM.SYS is also supplied with Windows 3 but if you use MS-DOS 5 you must use the version supplied with the operating system rather than the Windows one.

Devices

KEYBOARD.SYS

Defines the national characteristics of the keyboard, in essence it is the counterpart of COUNTRY.SYS.

SMARTDRV.SYS

A disk device which normally comes as part of Windows - although it was supplied as part of MS-DOS 4.0 on the machine I am using to write this.

Memory

Arguably this is the most important part of the computer system - without memory nothing will work. (A bit like people really!) All computers use two different types of memory, ROM and RAM. In actual fact both of these are part of the same memory chip, usually, but they are always referred to separately.

ROM is the acronym for Read Only Memory and that is exactly what it is. The ROM contains certain bits and pieces that the computer must have to operate correctly, such as the POST procedure, but which cannot be changed - hence the name.

On the other hand the RAM, Random Access Memory, changes constantly. It is into the RAM that all applications programs are loaded and where they run. All data you create is held here until you write to the disk, and any memory resident software you use resides here. In many computers the details of the machine's configuration are also stored in the RAM, albeit a different area of it. The amount of RAM you have and its health directly affect the computer's performance.

Most of today's AT's come complete with 1 or even 2 Mb of RAM, and this can usually be increased to around 16 Mb. That is a lot of memory - no matter which way you look at it - especially as MS-DOS will not allow you to use more than 640 Kb for running programs. The 640 Kb limit is a hangover from the earliest days of MS-DOS. When the operating system was created, the average memory of the machines it would run on was 64 Kb and therefore applying a maximum limit of ten times that seemed to be ample.

Assume that you have an AT with 4 Mb of RAM. What are you going to do with it? Currently your choice is severely limited:

Memory

- You can ignore that part above the 640 Kb limit, which is a bit silly considering you paid for it.

- You can use the extra memory as a disk cache. This allows the computer to memorise the locations of the most frequently used files so that they can be found and accessed faster. This is fine if you have a complex directory structure but a bit pointless if you have a well organised and tidy disk. Granted the disk cache will speed up disk access but you are unlikely to notice the effects unless you are using very disk-intensive software like a DTP program or one that uses a large number of overlays.

- The extra RAM can be used as a pseudo disk drive - a Ramdrive. This works in the same way as an ordinary disk drive but it is incredibly fast because it has no moving parts: it is totally electronic. The biggest problem with ramdrives is that they are only viable while the computer has power. Once you turn the machine off the contents of the ramdrive will be lost. (If you do intend using a ramdrive make sure you copy the contents of it onto the hard disk before you turn the computer off.)

- You can use Windows 3 which needs loads of memory to run properly.

In actuality what you do is use all of the above which gives you the best response.

Part Four
Installation

Getting ready

The MS-DOS 5.0 upgrade has one of the simplest and easiest to use installation routines you will ever come across - it is even better than the Windows one. However, before you begin using it there are some things that you should do first if only to give you peace of mind later. You don't have to do all of the following but if you do you always have a backup position to get yourself out of any problems.

The first thing to do is make an emergency boot disk based on the operating system you already have installed. This is very easy to as you only need to use two commands.

1   Boot your machine as normal and then take a floppy disk that is clean, either an old one that you no longer want or, preferably, a brand new one. Ideally the disk wants to go into Drive-A. (Some computers won't let you boot off of Drive-B!)

2   Enter **FORMAT A:/S**. What you are doing is formatting the floppy disk, so that it is readable by MS-DOS, and transferring the system files onto that disk. The reason you reformat the disk if you are using an old one is to make sure that there is nothing else on it. The computer will respond with:

Insert floppy disk into Drive-A
Press any key when ready...

Getting ready

3   As you already have the disk in the drive you can just press any key and the process begins. As the disk is formatted you get a running commentary on how much of it is already done, e.g. **52 percent completed**, until it is finished. The message then changes to **Format complete System transferred** followed by:

  Volume label (11 characters, ENTER for none)?

You are being asked to give the floppy disk a name. You can use any of the valid characters and, the only time you are allowed to do so, you can use blank spaces. So, for instance, you could call the disk **Fall Back 1**. Give the disk any name you wish and then press **Enter** or if you don't want to name it just press **Enter** by itself.

4   You then get another message which says something like:

   1213952 bytes total disk space
   119800   bytes used by system
   1094144 bytes available on disk

   512 bytes in each allocation unit.
   2137 allocation units available on disk.

   Volume Serial Number is 2E36-1EFE
   Format another (Y/N)?

Getting ready

The exact message will depend on which version of MS-DOS you are using at the moment. For example, the Volume Serial Number only appears on MS-DOS 4.0 and not with Version 3.30. You don't want to format another disk so press **N Enter** and you go back to the system prompt.

The disk you have just formatted can be used as a boot disk as it stands. It contains the main system files but none of the external commands and no configuration information. Ideally you want to be able to boot your system from the floppy as if you were booting it from the hard disk. So let's copy some files from your hard disk to the floppy before doing anything else.

5   Make sure you are in the root directory by entering **CD** and then enter **COPY AUTOEXEC.BAT A:** followed by **COPY CONFIG.SYS A:**. That's the main two files you need but you also want to include some of the MS-DOS external files to the floppy as well so that if necessary you can actually operate the computer directly from the floppy disk.

6   Change to the MS-DOS directory, e.g. enter **CD\DOS**, and then enter **DIR/W** to list the files there and find out how much room you need to store them on the floppy. You will find that there are too many files, occupying too much room, to fit onto a single floppy disk. You have two choices; either (a) you copy all the files but use two floppies, or (b) you copy selected

92

Getting ready

files. The choice is yours. Personally I always use the former option.

7   The files you particularly want to copy are those that you will be using most. I suggest the following:

ATTRIB	BACKUP	CHKDSK
COUNTRY.SYS	DISKCOPY	FDISK
FORMAT	HIMEM.SYS	KEYB
KEYBOARD	LABEL	RAMDRIVE.SYS
RESTORE	SHARE	SYS
TREE		

You don't have to have all these but there is sufficient here to cover most eventualities. Copy each file to the floppy by entering **COPY [FILENAME] A:**.

Once the files have been copied, write a label for the disk and then put it into a safe place. Never use this disk for anything else. Its sole purpose is to be used when you cannot boot off your hard disk.

8   Now copy the master disks as mentioned in Section 5 if you have not already done so. The final step is to make a clean, newly formatted floppy disk that the installation will need. Just put a floppy disk, preferably new, into Drive-A and enter **FORMAT A:**. The floppy must be one that fits into Drive-A - you cannot use Drive-B - at least not with the MS-DOS 5.0 upgrade kit that this book is written around.

Installing MS-DOS 5.0

The installation itself is simple, just follow the steps below and the on-screen prompts that will appear. I have written this chapter based around using a machine with 4 MB of RAM, a 64 Mb hard disk and a VGA monitor. Because of this certain parts of what follows may be slightly different to what you will see on your system. However, the differences will be negligible.

1   Place the copy of the first master disk into the floppy drive, it can be either Drive-A or Drive-B, and then log onto the drive by entering the drive letter followed by a colon. Then enter **SETUP**.

2   You will be presented with a full-screen message telling you what will happen. To begin the actual installation press **Enter**. You now get another message screen asking if you are using a network. As this book is written assuming you are using a stand-alone machine, press **N** to continue.

3   The MS-DOS 5.0 installation provides you with a facility for backing up your hard disk before the installation begins. Whether or not you do this depends on two factors. If you maintain a proper backup procedure, as you should do when using a hard disk, then you do not need to do this. On the other hand if you do not, and you want to continue living dangerously, then you can skip the backup.

Installing MS-DOS 5.0

If you do decide to backup your hard disk at this stage then the installation program will give you an indication of how many floppy disks, of various sizes, you will need to do so. For example, one of the machines that is being used for this book uses a 64 Mb hard disk. According to the setup program I will need:

    137 360 Kb disks, or
      69 720 Kb disks, or
      41 1.20 Mb disks, or
      35 1.44 Mb disks.

As I don't have that many spare floppy disks available at the moment I chose not to backup the hard disk. The number of disks you will need depends on how large your hard disk is and how many files you have on it.

4   Once the backup is done, if you are doing it, or once you decide not to do so, Setup will then examine your system and try to determine how it is configured and how the new MS-DOS should be installed for it. This 'guessing' will be right 99.99% of the time. The table will look something like this:

DOS Type   **:MS-DOS**
DOS Path   **:C:\DOS**
MS-DOS Shell:Do no run MS-DOS Shell on startup.
Display Type :VGA

Installing MS-DOS 5.0

You have the option of changing any of the above. You can use the **Up** and **Down** cursor keys to move the highlighter bar to any option and then press **Enter** to change it. If you do so you will be presented with different options to select from. For the purposes of this chapter I selected to accept the options above.

5   You are then given a final chance to change your mind before the actual installation begins. Once the installation process starts you cannot stop it except by turning off the power - a situation that will do untold damage to your system. Pressing **Y** begins the process of upgrading the system.

6   From here on it is simply a question of responding to the messages that will appear on the screen. Early on you will be asked to place a floppy disk into Drive-A (You cannot use Drive-B!) onto which the existing operating system and its files that are on your hard disk will be transferred. They are also backed up on your hard disk itself into a new directory called OLD_DOS. You will be shown a moving bar graph of the progress of the installation as it unfolds. Thereafter it is just a case of swapping disks when prompted to do so.

7   Finally you get a message telling you that the setup is complete and asking you to press **Enter** to start MS-DOS 5.0. Doing so will restart you system as if

Installing MS-DOS 5.0

you had pressed **Ctrl-Alt-Del**. Make sure you remove any disks from the floppy drives before you do so.

If you check your MS-DOS directory you will find that it now contains 88 files that take up 2141628 bytes of disk space.

Tidying up

There is one special file installed by setup called DELOLDOS.EXE. This file will delete the backup copies of the old operating system off your hard disk. I suggest that you do not use it for a while. Give yourself a couple of months to get used to the new version of the operating system and then you can get rid of the old one.

When you are ready to remove the old system just enter **DELOLDOS** and the command does the rest. It will delete all the files from OLD_DOS.1, remove the directory itself and then erase itself from your hard disk. Nice and neat.

There are two TXT files in the MS-DOS directory that you should read:

> **APPNOTES** contains information about using MS-DOS 5.0 with various third party programs and other software. Read it to see if any of it applies to your system. Thereafter you can delete it.

> **README** is much longer and is concerned with systems and specific software packages. It contains information that could not be included in the manual, or the help system, and so you should read it.

To read either of the files above I suggest that you enter **TYPE APPNOTES.TXT |MORE** or **TYPE README.TXT |MORE**.

The |MORE part of the command will present the files in chunks of 23 lines at a time so you can read it at leisure. To move to the next screen you simply press any key.

Part Five
Configuration

Using memory

The major advance that MS-DOS 5.0 contains is that it allows you to configure your usage of memory. When you install the operating system it will create a CONFIG.SYS and AUTOEXEC.BAT as it thinks they should be. This will work very well but you can tweak both files to get better performance from the system. Before you do that though it helps if you understand something about the way that memory works and what the various parts of it are. There are essentially four types of memory.

Conventional Memory

All computers contain conventional memory - they have to. Regardless of how much RAM your system has, and today's computers can come complete with anything from 1 Mb (1,024 KB) to 16 Mb (16,384 Kb) it is more usual for them to have about 4 MB (4,084 Kb). The conventional memory is that part of the RAM that occupies the first 640 Kb of the available memory. If you had only 512 Kb of memory then it would all be conventional memory.

The vast majority of programs you will run on your system will use the conventional memory area. Therefore it follows that the more conventional memory you can make available, the more programs you can run at the same time. However, any device driver you use will use some of the conventional memory area and so that cuts down the available amount. Whatever is left after you have added these is what is available for running programs. By tweaking the CONFIG.SYS and AUTOEXEC.BAT you should be able to get around 600 Kb of free conventional memory!

Using memory

Upper Memory Area

The next part of the memory is that part that lies between the conventional memory at 640 Kb and the start of the extended memory at 1,024 Kb. With every version of MS-DOS prior to 5.0 this was largely wasted. Granted some device drivers and some third party programs could occupy it but on the whole it was wasted. The unused part of the upper memory area are called UMB's - Upper Memory Blocks.

If you are using a computer that is based around the 80386 or 80486 chip then you can access these UMB's to place device drivers there, for example, and so free more of the conventional memory area.

Extended Memory (XMS)

Extended memory is that part of the RAM that lies above the 1,024 Kb base area. You can only have extended memory on a computer that uses an 80286 chip or higher because it needs to tie into the standard mode of the chip itself. Generally speaking all computers based on the 80286 chip and beyond will have at least 1 Mb of RAM.

The majority of programs that use conventional memory cannot use extended memory. (The major exception to this is Microsoft Windows.) The reason for this is that programs are not designed to use it.

To use the extended memory you need a program called an extended memory manager the purpose of which is to prevent

Using memory

two programs trying to use the same memory area at the same time. MS-DOS comes complete with just such a program - called HIMEM.SYS.

By the way, if you are using Windows and you upgrade to MS-DOS 5.0 you must use the HIMEM.SYS that comes with MS-DOS 5.0 and not the one supplied with Windows. The one that comes with the operating system is newer and better.

Expanded Memory (EMS)

Expanded memory is the another way of adding memory to your system. This consists of a board which you have to add to the system and an expanded memory manager program. Some programs work with expanded memory while others are unable to do so. All expanded memory boards must conform to a standard called LIM EMS which determines how program use expanded memory.

In order to use memory efficiently you need to use memory manager programs. This is a special type of device driver that provides access to the extra memory on your system. MS-DOS 5.0 comes complete with two such programs.

HIMEM.SYS

This is the device driver that allows you to access the extended memory areas. It has to be installed in the CONFIG.SYS before anything else. HIMEM.SYS has advantages and disadvantages

Using memory

but the former far outweigh the latter especially as the only real disadvantage is that the program may not be compatible with very old software, for example Windows 286. (In this case very old means more than about 2 years!)

EMM386.EXE

This is the program that allows access to the upper memory area. It can also be used to simulate expanded memory in extended memory. Note that it does not replace any EMS manager, that is dependent on the type of expanded memory board you are using. You can only use EMM386 if you are using an 80386 or 80486 based machine.

Again the version of EMM386 that comes with MS-DOS 5.0 supersedes the one that comes with Windows 3.0 and so you must use the newer one. In addition you cannot use EMM386 is you are using another expanded memory manager.

Using resources

For the purposes of this chapter I installed MS-DOS 5.0 onto my smaller machine. This is a Laser 80386 with 2 Mb of RAM. Before I started I deleted the original AUTOEXEC.BAT and the CONFIG.SYS. The setup routine created the following files, what the lines mean are covered in the next section:

CONFIG.SYS

> DEVICE=C:\DOS\SETVER.SYS
> DEVICE=C:\DOS\HIMEM.SYS
> DOS=HIGH
> FILES=10
> SHELL=C:\DOS\COMMAND.COM C:\DOS\ /P

AUTOEXEC.BAT

> @ECHO OFF
> PROMPT PG
> PATH C:\DOS
> SET TEMP=C:\DOS

MS-DOS 5.0 comes with a command called MEM, which gives a report on memory usage, and by entering this I get a report that says:

> 655360 bytes total conventional memory
> 655360 bytes available to MS-DOS
> 637808 largest executable program size

Using resources

1441792 bytes total contiguous extended memory
0 bytes available contiguous extended memory
1376256 bytes available XMS memory
MS-DOS resident in High Memory Area

But what does all this mean?

- The 655360 conventional memory is the maximum amount it can be, i.e. 640 Kb.

- The 655360 available to MS-DOS is the same.

- Largest executable program size is the amount of conventional memory that is left after the basic operating system is loaded. The total is 622.9 Kb. Remember that at this point there is no real configuration in place, e.g. the national characteristics are missing.

- The first line of the second part tells you that there is 1408 Kb of extended memory available. Add the conventional memory to that and you get the 2 Mb that is fitted to the machine.

- The 0 bytes bit, which alarms many people, simply tells you that the extended memory is not currently being managed and so the value is zero.

- Available XMS memory is the amount of extended memory that is available to those programs which can use it. In this case 1,344 Kb.

So that is what we have to work with. Now let's get on with it.

Editing files

The first thing that we have to do is begin the customisation of the operating system. To start with we will just add the country specific bits to the CONFIG.SYS and the AUTOEXEC.BAT. Changing either of these files has always been a bit of a pain in previous versions of MS-DOS, but Version 5.0 includes a new program called EDIT which makes life much easier.

Edit is a simple text editor that operates much the same as Windows Notepad. It is actually a part of QBASIC.EXE and if you delete that file then you cannot use Edit. To use the program you simply enter **EDIT** which will activate the text editor. However, you can use a command line input and enter **EDIT [FILENAME]** directly from the system prompt which will run the Edit program and automatically load the required file into it for you.

1. Make sure you are in the root directory by entering **CD** and then enter **EDIT CONFIG.SYS**. The text editor will run and the file is loaded automatically.

Before going any further let's take a look at what the lines in the existing CONFIG.SYS mean. Notice that some lines contain the full path to where a program resides on your hard disk.

DEVICE=C:\DOS\SETVER.EXE

SETVER is used to identify the operating system to various programs. Why? Some programs are very finicky about what versions of MS-DOS you use them with and as MS-DOS 5.0 is brand new there are very few programs that have been modified

Editing files

to use it effectively. The result is that you use SETVER to fool the programs into thinking they are using the version of MS-DOS that they want. You can also add to or delete from the SETVER table. (See the appropriate section in Chapter 6 for full details.)

DEVICE=C:\DOS\HIMEM.SYS

HIMEM is the memory manager that allows access to the higher reaches of the RAM as we've already discussed.

DOS=HIGH

This line loads the basic operating system into the high memory area. Without this line the amount of free conventional memory would be reduced to 589,392 bytes - a loss of 48,416 bytes or nearly 48 Kb.

FILES=10

This lines tells the operating system how many files it can have open at any one time. The actual number depends on the kind of application program you are using. 10, which is what the setup set this line to, is extremely low considering that the minimum has to be at least 8! You would expect the value to be in the range 20 to 30.

Editing files

SHELL=C:\DOS\COMMAND.COM C:\DOS\ /P

This line tells the operating system where to find the command interpreter. If you want to place COMMAND.COM anywhere other that in the root then you need this line. If you leave COMMAND.COM in the root then you can omit it.

As every device you load uses memory you can recover some of the RAM by keeping devices to a minimum.

2   MS-DOS 5.0 allows you to place REM statements in front of lines that you are unsure about keeping. By placing REM at the beginning of a line, anything that line contains will not be acted upon. SETVER is not really necessary - at least I have yet to find a program that will not work if this line is missing. So place REM in from of it.

3   Change the number of FILES to 30. (You can move around the file by using the cursor keys.) Then place a REM statement in from of the last line - assuming that you have COMMAND.COM in your root directory. If you don't have then you cannot change this line.

4   You can close the text editor by pressing **Alt-F X**. A message box appears telling you that the loaded file has not been saved and giving you the option to do

Editing files

so. Just press **Enter** and the file will be saved and the editor closed so you drop back to the system prompt.

5   Reboot the system by pressing **Ctrl-Alt-Del**.

6   Enter **MEM** and you will find that the amount of available memory has dropped to 637,056 bytes - a reduction of 752 bytes on the original configuration. The extra memory has gone to the FILES statement because each additional file uses some of the RAM.

7   Now let us add the first part of the national characteristics, the other part will go into the AUTOEXEC.BAT. Enter **EDIT CONFIG.SYS** again. When the file is loaded you have to add a new line to the end of the file. Move the cursor to the bottom of the file by pressing **Ctrl-End** or repeatedly press **Down** and then type **COUNTRY=044,,C:\DOS\COUNTRY.SYS**. That sets the computer to the UK standard. Oddly, adding this line to the CONFIG.SYS does not reduce the amount of memory available.

8   There is one very important thing missing from the file - the BUFFERS statement. This is necessary and it is odd that setup did not set any. Add a line saying **BUFFERS=10** after the FILES line. This is not very many, for a system with 640 Kb of conventional memory the default should be 15 but as the buffers

109

Editing files

are a 'poor man's disk cache' and we are going to add a better one, the value of 10 is sufficient. Besides which each buffer used 532 bytes of the memory so we want as few as possible.

9   Let's add the disk cache program next. Add a line saying **DEVICE=C:\DOS\SMARTDRV.SYS 1024 512** before the FILES line but after the one saying DOS=HIGH. Smartdrv is the MS-DOS disk cache, again you must use the one that comes with MS-DOS rather the one that comes with Windows.

What do the values mean? The first number, in this case 1024, is the initial maximum size that the disk cache can be. The second is the smallest size it can be.

10 Close the text editor and save the file by pressing **Alt-F X Enter**. Now reboot the machine, again by pressing **Ctrl-Alt-Del**, to activate the changes you have made.

If you enter **MEM** now you will get the following report:

Editing files

> 655360 bytes total conventional memory
> 655360 bytes available to MS-DOS
> 618448 largest executable program size
>
> 1441792 bytes total contiguous extended memory
>   0 bytes available contiguous extended memory
> 327680 bytes available XMS memory
>   **MS-DOS resident in High Memory Area**

In other words the amount of conventional memory has been reduced to just under 604 Kb and the amount of XMS memory is down by 1,024 Kb - the size of the SMARTDRV cache. On a machine with only 2 MB of RAM this is a major reduction - in fact it's too much particularly if you are running Windows 3. I've just checked this by trying to run Windows with these new settings and I am reduced to using Standard Mode. As I want to use Enhanced Mode I have to change the Smartdrv parameters.

11 Enter **EDIT CONFIG.SYS** again. Let's rearrange the whole file while we're at it. Move the cursor to the Files line. Hold down **Shift** and then press **Down** twice. The files and buffers lines will both be highlighted. Now press **Shift-Del** and the lines will be cut, i.e. they vanish into the memory. Move the cursor to the top of the file by pressing **Shift-Home** and then press **Shift-Ins** and the two lines will be pasted into place. In the same way move the two REM lines down to the bottom of the file.

111

Editing files

12 Change the values for Smartdrv to 512 256. You should now have something like this:

> **FILES=30**
> **BUFFERS=10**
> **DEVICE=C:\DOS\HIMEM.SYS**
> **DOS=HIGH**
> **DEVICE=C:\DOS\SMARTDRV.SYS 512 256**
> **COUNTRY=044,,C:\DOS\COUNTRY.SYS**
> **REM DEVICE=C:\DOS\SETVER.SYS**
> **SHELL=C:\DOS\COMMAND.COM C:\DOS\ /P**

Before doing anything else save the amended file by pressing **Alt-F S**. Now we can make some changes to the Autoexec.

13 Press **Alt-F O** and a dialogue box appears. The File Name line has ***.TXT** highlighted in it. Enter **AUTOEXEC.BAT** and the file will be loaded into the editor. The file says:

> **@ECHO OFF**
> **PROMPT PG**
> **PATH C:\DOS**
> **SET TEMP=C:\DOS**

Editing files

14 The one thing we have to add is the keyboard driver that will allow you to get a £ sign rather than # amongst other things. Move the cursor to the bottom of the file and then type **C:\DOS\KEYB UK,, C:\DOS\KEYBOARD.SYS**. This is the complement to COUNTRY.SYS and sets the keyboard to a UK one.

15 Press **Alt-F X Enter** to close the editor again and save the file. Then reboot using **Ctrl-Alt-Del**.

16 When the machine has rebooted type **MEM** and you will find that you have 612,768 bytes of conventional memory. This means that we now have, roughly, 598 Kb of conventional memory as opposed to the 623 we originally had. So what we have done so far has used up 25 Kb of RAM. This is still much less than you would have had if you were using MS-DOS 4.0 but we can do better thanks to the way that MS-DOS 5.0 allows you to place things into the high memory area.

Freeing memory

You can see how the operating system is using memory if you enter **MEM/C**. The /C is short for Classify and it is one of the parameters that can be applied to the command. (Details of the other are in the appropriate section in Part 6.) This will give you list of how the memory is allocated, something like this:

Conventional Memory:

Name	Size in Decimal		Size in Hex
MSDOS	14144	(13.8K)	3740
HIMEM	1184	(1.2K)	4A0
SMARTDRV	18048	(17.6K)	4680
COMMAND	2624	(2.6K)	A40
KEYB	6208	(6.1K)	1840
FREE	64	(0.1K)	40
FREE	80	(0.1K)	50
FREE	612768	(598.4K)	959A0
Total FREE	612912	(598.5K)	

Total bytes available to programs: 612912 (598.5K)
Largest executable program size: 612768 (598.4K)

  1441792 bytes total contiguous extended memory
        0 bytes available contiguous extended memory
   851968 bytes available XMS memory
          MS-DOS resident in High Memory Area

The point about this is that you are using HIMEM and so you can access the high memory area but as yet there is nothing there. So let's put something into it.

Freeing memory

1. In order to get into the HMA you need to add a parameter to the DOS=HIGH command. So enter **EDIT CONFIG.SYS** again. Move the cursor down to the end of the DOS line and add **,UMB** to the end of it. You must include the comma. That's part one. You also need to load a new device driver and this must be added to the CONFIG.SYS immediately after the DOS=HIGH,UMB line.

2. Move the cursor down one line and then type **DEVICE=C:\DOS\EMM386.EXE NOEMS** followed by **Enter** so that this becomes a new line. The NOEMS means no EMS and so you are stating that you are not going to use Expanded Memory.

3. Press **Alt-F X Enter** to close the text editor and save the file. Then reboot the system by pressing **Ctrl-Alt-Del** again. When the system comes back on-line enter **MEM/C** again and you will find things are different.

You are now using the Upper Memory Area and can see it. The total bytes available to programs is now 670.3 Kb but the largest executable program size has been reduced to 590.2 Kb. The reason is that you added a new device driver and so some memory is lost. Never fear, you're about to get it back.

Freeing memory

4   Enter **EDIT CONFIG.SYS** again. Move the cursor down to the line that contains Smartdrv and change it to read **DEVICEHIGH=C:\DOS\SMARTDRV.SYS 512 256**. This will load the cache into the high memory area. Unfortunately you cannot load HIMEM or EMM386 into the high memory area, they have to stay in conventional memory.

5   Save the file by pressing **Alt-F S**. Then load the Autoexec again. Press **Alt-F O** and a dialogue box appears. The File Name line has ***.TXT** highlighted in it. Enter **AUTOEXEC.BAT** and the file will be loaded into the editor.

6   Move the cursor down to the beginning of the last line, the one containing the keyboard driver. Add **LH** to the beginning of the line, leaving a space between the letter and C:. The letters stand for Load High and means that this driver will also go into the High Memory Area.

7   Close the editor, **Alt-F X**, and then reboot the system a final time. Enter **MEM/C** again once the machine is back on line and you will find that you have increased the Largest executable program size to 613.9 Kb - almost as much as we had at the beginning. In fact we have only used 9 Kb more.

Freeing memory

But look at the difference. You now have:

a) Two of the device drivers loaded into the high memory area, even if you have had to leave two of them in conventional memory.

b) You have a disk cache that will speed up all future disk access times.

c) Your computer system will run Windows 3.0 in 386-Enhanced mode.

d) The machine is configured for the UK.

All in all that's not bad and you still have more free memory than you would have had using any previous version of MS-DOS.

Using 8 Mb of RAM

The foregoing section referred to a machine with only 2 Mb of RAM - what you might call a Minimum Windows Machine. (I use Windows for at least 95% of my work. For example, this book is being written in Word for Windows - as are all my books - and it will be set in PageMaker. All the graphics I do are done in CorelDRAW and so on. As far as I am concerned Windows 3 is the best thing since someone thought of chopping the corners off square wheels!)

The main machine I use is an Arche Pro-File 80486. This currently has 8 Mb of RAM on board, but will soon have 16 Mb, and a 340 Mb SCSI hard disk. I need the sheer power and speed that this system gives me but am willing to admit that most people don't. However, for those who are interested here is how the big system is configured.

CONFIG.SYS

```
FILES=30
BUFFERS=10
LASTDRIVE=J
DEVICE=C:\DOS\HIMEM.SYS
DOS=HIGH,UMB
DEVICE=C:\DOS\EMM386.EXE NOEMS
DEVICEHIGH=C:\DOS\RAMDRIVE.SYS 2560/E
DEVICEHIGH=C:\DOS\SMARTDRV.SYS 2048 1024
DEVICEHIGH=C:\DOS\SETVER.EXE
COUNTRY=044,,C:\DOS\COUNTRY.SYS
```

The big difference here is that I use a Ramdrive of 2.5 Mb, which is Drive-J because the hard disk is partitioned into seven logical drives. The ramdrive is used for temporary file storage when

Using 8 Mb of RAM

running Windows and this combined with the large Smartdrv means that, effectively, Windows is speeded up some 30%.

AUTOEXEC.BAT

```
@ECHO OFF
CLS
PATH=C:\;C:\DOS;C:\BELFRY;C:\UTILITYS;D:\WINDOWS;
D:\WINWORD;D:\EXCEL;D:\ALDUS;D:\PM4
PROMPT $P$G
LH C:\DOS\KEYB UK,,C:\DOS\KEYBOARD.SYS
LH C:\DOS\DOSKEY.COM
VERIFY ON
MD J:\TEMP
SET TEMP=J:\TEMP
CLS
PATH
DIR/W
```

Exactly how you configure your machine is purely a matter of personal taste. The previous section and this one are intended to give you guide lines of what I have found to work best on my systems.

The interesting thing is that on the 80486 the amount of conventional memory space used by MSDOS is 15,392 bytes while on the 80386 it only uses 14,160 bytes. On an 80286 it uses even less! However, the amount of Upper Memory space used by the System remains the same on all systems.

119

Part Six

Commands

Types of commands

This chapter will contain details of every operating system command that there is within MS-DOS 5.0, including a full description of the command, details of its use, its parameters where they apply and example of how to use the command.

The important point to realise is that all the commands can be categorised in different ways. MS-DOS contains internal and external commands, as we have already discovered, the former being part of COMMAND.COM and the latter being distinct programs in their own right. In addition some commands can be used directly from the system prompt while others have to be installed in some way, usually within the CONFIG.SYS. Then there are the Batch file commands. I had to decide whether or not to include this last category within this chapter or keep them for their own chapter. In the end I have decided that as this chapter is intended to be an alphabetical listing of all the available commands, the full details of the batch commands would be included here and shortened particulars in the batch file chapter.

As a result of this each command will be laid out in the same fashion as follows:

> The running head at the top of each page gives the command name, with an extension where appropriate for external commands. For those commands that are internal ones no extension will be given.
>
> The first line of each section will then tell you the type of command that is involved, i.e.

■ Operating System   ❐ Batch File   ❐ Configuration

Types of commands

where the black square denotes which type of command this is. Where there is a special notation for the batch file commands it means that those commands will normally only be used with batch files and not from the system prompt.

a. Description of the command, what it does and any other information about it.

b. Command syntax, i.e. how you have to use it.

c. Parameter information, where necessary, about what the various parameters do.

d. Examples of using the command and the expected result from the written usage.

e. Error messages. Any specific error message associated with a command will be given. There is also a generic error message, **Bad command or filename**, which generally means that you have asked for a command that is not accessible or you have mis-spelled it.

f. Special notes. Containing specific information about the command.

MS-DOS 5.0 does provide a certain amount of help about some of the various commands it contains. You can access this from the system prompt by entering the command name followed by **/?**. Unfortunately the information you get is very brief but it may be enough to get you out of a tight corner.

ANSI.SYS

☐ Operating System   ☐ Batch file   ■ Configuration

Description

ANSI.SYS is a device driver and as such it must be installed in the CONFIG.SYS file. It can be loaded into the High Memory Area. Its purpose is to allow you to change the functions of various parts of the computer system, notably the screen display and keyboard.

Command syntax

DEVICE=[DRIVE:] [PATH] **ANSI.SYS** [/x] [/K]

Parameter information

[DRIVE:][PATH] Specifies the drive and path to the location of the device driver.

[/x] Used only for systems with 101 or 102-key keyboards. On such keyboards there are, effectively, two sets of cursor control keys, one set lying between the main keyboard and the numeric keypad and the other being on the numeric keypad. By using the /x switch the numeric keypad can be reassigned.

[/K] Ignores the extended keys on 101 and 102-key keyboards.

ANSI.SYS

Commands examples

1. To load the standard device driver without any parameters you would include a line in your CONFIG.SYS saying **DEVICE=C:\DOS\ANSI.SYS**.

2. To ignore the second set of cursor control keys you would use the command in the CONFIG.SYS as **DEVICE=C:\DOS\ANSI.SYS /K**.

Error Messages

There are no specific error messages for this command.

Notes

a. These days **ANSI.SYS** is rarely used but you may find that some old software requires the device driver to be loaded so that the programs can write to the screen correctly.

APPEND.EXE

■ Operating System ◻ Batch file ◻ Configuration

Description

APPEND allows you to set a search path for data files in specific directories as if the data files were within the current directory. Normally only used on networked systems to allow users to share the same data. In fact it is very similar to the PATH command: you can specify any directory and/or drive that is valid under normal MS-DOS rules.

Command syntax

APPEND [DRIVE:] [PATH] [;] [/X [:ON or :OFF]] [/PATH:ON or /PATH:OFF] [/E]

Parameter information:

[DRIVE:][PATH] Specifies the drive and path that is to be appended to the current directory.

[;] You can specify multiple drives and paths by separating each one with a semi-colon. If you enter the semi-colon by itself then you will cancel all existing appended directories.

[/X:ON] Tells the command that it can search appended directories for files when executing programs. Some application programs depend on having the full path specified and so they cannot normally be used with the **APPEND** command - with the command active the application might hang up. However, by

APPEND.EXE

invoking the /x parameter, some of these, at this point, of these will then work correctly.

[/X:OFF] This is the default which tells the command not to search appended directories when executing programs. The directories will be searched only for data files to be opened.

[/PATH:ON] Specifies that the program can also search any path that is included with the name of the program. This is the default.

[/PATH:OFF] Specifies that the program may not search named paths for files.

[/E] Allows you to store a copy of the list of appended directories to a variable called APPEND. You can only use this switch the first time that you run the command. You must run the command as **APPEND /E** first and then use it again specifying the directories and parameters you want to use.

Command examples:

1   To check the current status of the command just enter it without specifying any parameters, i.e. **APPEND**, and the computer will respond with a message, e.g. **APPEND already installed**.

2   When you have finished with it you can cancel the command - but not remove it - by entering **APPEND;**. This will clear the search path that you originally

APPEND.EXE

specified, i.e. set a null path, so that MS-DOS only searches the current directory as it would normally. The **APPEND** command cannot be uninstalled except by rebooting the machine.

3   Once the command is in operation, i.e. you have specified a search path, then whenever you request a data file MS-DOS will search through the current directory, regardless of whether or not it is part of the APPEND command, and then search each of the specified locations in the order they are given to try and find the data file you requested.

4   If you wish to allow a program to access files in a directory called Alpha on Drive-E and those in a directory named Beta on Drive-C you would use the command as **APPEND F:\ALPHA;C:\BETA**.

Error Messages

Using an incorrect parameter will bring up the message **Invalid switch - [character]**.

APPEND.EXE

Notes

a. The advantage to using **APPEND** really only lies with networked systems: for instance you can access data from remote directories and it is not intended to be used on stand-alone systems. If you want to use **ASSIGN** as well, then **APPEND** must be used first.

b. When using DIR you will not be given a listing of the files in the appended directories, only the directory that you are logged on to at the time you execute the command.

c. If you have two files bearing the same name, but stored in different directories, then the program looking for the file will open the file that is in the current directory or in the first named directory.

d. When you save files when using append and you do not specify a full path to the file you want to save, the program will write the file to the current directory - even if the original copy of that file came from an appended directory.

ASSIGN.COM

■ **Operating System**   ☐ **Batch file**   ☐ **Configuration**

Description

ASSIGN allows you to treat one disk drive as if it were another, i.e. it allows you to fool the computer into believing that one drive does not exist. For instance, suppose you had just a single floppy machine but you were using software that demanded you had two floppies. In the normal course of events you then have two options: (a) Get rid of the software, or (b) Cheat and use ASSIGN.

Command Syntax

> **ASSIGN** [DRIVE1] = [DRIVE2]

or

> **ASSIGN**/STATUS

Parameter Information

> [DRIVE1] is the drive which is being assigned from.
>
> [DRIVE2] is the drive which is being assigned to.
>
> /STATUS will display a list of currently operable assignments. Can be shortened to /STA or just /S.

ASSIGN.COM

Command Examples

1   To use software that insists on having both Drive-A and Drive-B when you only have a single floppy you would use the command as **ASSIGN B=A**.

Note that you do not have to include the colon that normally follows a drive designator. What this effectively does is to tell MS-DOS that every time the application program wants to use Drive-B it reads or writes to Drive-A instead. You must remember that the drive to be used always goes after the equals sign.

2   You can use ASSIGN to devolve any drive. For instance if you enter **ASSIGN A=C B=C D=C E=C** then only Drive-C can be used - the others are effectively not there as far as an application program or MS-DOS itself are concerned. To include multiple drives in this way you simply separate each one by a space as shown.

3   To cancel the assignations at any time just enter **ASSIGN** without specifying any drives, this returns everything to normal and the various drives resume their correct places.

ASSIGN.COM

Error Messages

There are no specific error messages for this command though you will get **Invalid switch** if you use the wrong letters.

Notes

a. If you wish to use the APPEND command and ASSIGN then the former must be used first. Equally you should not use ASSIGN with those commands that require drive information, e.g. BACKUP, LABEL, JOIN, RESTORE, PRINT and SUBST.

b. You cannot assign your hard disk to another drive though you can do it the other way round. For example, **ASSIGN C=A** is invalid while **ASSIGN A=C** is not.

c. You cannot use ASSIGN with nonexistent drives. For example you cannot have **ASSIGN J=C** if your system does not have Drive-J.

d. You can use ASSIGN on networked drives.

e. If you reassign drives it cancels the previous assignation. Thus if you originally had used **ASSIGN A=C** and then later entered **ASSIGN B=C** this will release Drive-A.

f. To cancel all assignments just enter **ASSIGN** by itself.

ATTRIB.EXE

■ Operating System ☐ Batch file ☐ Configuration

Description

Each file on your disks, regardless of the type, possesses a number of attributes, e.g. the size, date and time of creation. Some of these are visible whenever you use the **DIR** command - the exact number depends on the format you use for the command. But there are four other attributes which you do not normally see and which affect the way the file is handled by the computer and by other commands. **ATTRIB** allows you to see and change these. MS-DOS 5.0 allows you to also change the System and Hidden attributes - something that was not possible with previous versions of the operating system.

Command Syntax

> **ATTRIB** [PARAMETER(S)] [DRIVE:] [PATH] [FILENAME(S)] [/S]
>
> or
>
> **ATTRIB** [FILENAME(S)]

Parameter Information

ATTRIB allows you to turn attributes on or off by using a plus sign for the former and a minus sign for the latter. The sign must be placed in front of the letter of the attribute you want to change.

> **+A** Turns on the Archive attribute. This attribute denotes that a file has changed since it was previously backed up.

ATTRIB.EXE

-A Turns off the archive attribute so that a file will not be backed up.

+R Makes a file Read-only so that it cannot be changed.

-R Turns the Read-only attribute off.

+S Turns the file into a System one.

-S Makes System files accessible and visible.

+H Turns on the Hidden attribute so that a file is not visible when you use **DIR**.

-H Makes hidden files visible.

/S Allows you to use the command with all the files in a sub-directory.

Command Examples

1. If you enter **ATTRIB *.*** you will get a listing similar to the **DIR** listing, but without the size and date information and including the actual location of the file. However, each file will be preceded by one or two letters and the full path of the file, e.g.

    | A | R | C:\DOS\SHARE.EXE |
    | A | R | C:\DOS\SHELL.ASC |
    | | R | C:\DOS\SHELL.CLR |
    | | R | C:\DOS\SHELL.HLP |

ATTRIB.EXE

The first letter refers to the Archive bit. Every time that you create or modify any file this bit is turned on, so that the letter appears whenever you use the command as above. It is mainly used by programs that make backup copies of your files, including **BACKUP** itself. Whenever a file is backed up, the archive bit is turned off so that the computer knows which files have been duplicated and which haven't.

The second letter is the more important of the two as it refers to the file's ability to be changed or deleted. The **R** stands for Read Only and any file with this bit set cannot be erased or changed. It is useful to make all your system files Read Only as it will protect them from being accidentally erased, especially if you have a hard disk where the inadvertent use of **DEL *.*** could wreak havoc with your files.

2   If you enter **ATTRIB -a *.*** then you will turn off the Archive bit so that the file display changes, when you enter **ATTRIB *.*** again, to read:

        R   C:\DOS\SHARE.EXE
        R   C:\DOS\SHELL.ASC
        R   C:\DOS\SHELL.CLR
        R   C:\DOS\SHELL.HLP

ATTRIB.EXE

3 By entering **ATTRIB -r *.*** the display will read:

> C:\DOS\SHARE.EXE
> C:\DOS\SHELL.ASC
> C:\DOS\SHELL.CLR
> C:\DOS\SHELL.HLP

4 If, from the root directory, you enter **ATTRIB +R /s** then every single file on your hard disk will have its Read-Only attribute turned on. This may take some time depending on the size of your hard disk.

5 You can combine attributes into a single command string if you wish. For example, if you enter **ATTRIB +A +R +H /s** from the root directory then you will turn On the Archive attributes of every file on your hard disk, because of the **/s**, and make them Read-Only and hide them from view all at the same time.

Error Messages

There are no specific error messages for this command.

Notes

a. ATTRIB is one of the most important files on your system which is why I always include it on an emergency boot disk.

AUTOEXEC.BAT

☐ Operating System ☐ Batch file ■ Configuration

Description

The **AUTOEXEC.BAT** is one of the two files that you can create and/or modify to change the configuration information that your computer system operates under. The file is a pure ASCII one and as such can be changed using **EDIT** or any word or text processor that can produce pure ASCII files.

Command Syntax

There is no specific syntax for the AUTOEXEC.BAT as it simply contains a list of other commands and the syntax applies to them.

Parameter Information

Not applicable

Command Examples

Everyone's AUTOEXEC.BAT is liable to be different because it depends on what you want your system to do. See the next chapter for some sample files.

AUTOEXEC.BAT

Error Messages

Any error message will be generated by the commands in the AUTOEXEC.BAT rather than by the file itself.

Notes

a. You do not need to have an **AUTOEXEC.BAT** on your system. If you omit it then when the computer boots you will be asked to input the current time and date and your system will perform as an American machine. (The default for every computer world-wide.)

BACKUP.EXE

■ Operating System   ☐ Batch file   ☐ Configuration

Description

BACKUP is exactly what it says, a program that will create backup copies of your files onto floppy disks. It will backup all those files you specify, or those in the current directory if you do not specify a file type, that have their Archive bit set to on. If you have changed this, using either the **ATTRIB** command or a utility, then your files will not be backed up. Once a file has been backed up MS-DOS will automatically change the Archive attribute to off so that it knows which files have been backed up for future reference.

When you make a backup a special file is created on each of the floppies used, called **BACKUP.LOG**, which contains the details of the time and date of when the files were backed up, along with a list of all the files that were copied on that date and on which disk they are located.

Command Syntax

   BACKUP [SOURCE] [DESTINATION] [/S] [/M] [/A] [/F:SIZE] [/D:DATE] [/T:TIME] [/L[:[DRIVE:] [PATH] LOGFILE]]

Parameter Information

   [SOURCE] Specifies the directory and path from which files are to be backed up.

BACKUP.EXE

[DESTINATION:] Specifies the drive to which files are to be written. Note that you cannot specify a directory for the back-ups – only a drive.

/s Means that the command will backup the contents of all sub-directories that are sub-tended off the source directory.

/M Forces the command to backup only those files that changed since the last backup was made.

/A Adds back-ups to existing backup disks without deleting the original files.

/F:SIZE As you backup onto floppies these will be formatted, if necessary, to the maximum size possible in that floppy drive. However, you must have the **FORMAT** command available on your path. You can force the disks to be formatted to a different size by using this parameter. The possible sizes are:

> **160** Which can be written as 160, 160k or 160kb. Used for formatting 160 Kb, SSDD 5.25" disks.
>
> **180** Used for formatting 180 Kb, SSDD 5.25" disks. Can be written as 180, 180k or 180kb.
>
> **320** Used for formatting 320 Kb, DSDD 5.25" disks. Can be written as 320, 320k or 320kb.
>
> **360** Used for 360 Kb, DSDD 5.25" disks. Written as 360, 360k or 360kb.

BACKUP.EXE

720 Used to format 720 Kb DSDD 3.5" disks. Can be written as 720, 720k or 720kb.

1200 Used to format 1.2 Mb 5.25" disks. Can be written as 1200, 1200k, 1200kb, 1.2, 1.2m or 1.2mb.

1440 Used for 1.44Mb 3.5" floppies. Can be written as 1440, 1440k, 1440kb, 1.44, 1.44m or 1.44mb.

2880 Used for 2.88Mb 3.5" floppy disks. MS-DOS 5.0 is the first generally available operating system to make use of these new higher density floppies. Unfortunately the actual drives are hard to find. The number can be written as 2880, 2880k, 2880kb, 2.88, 2.88m or 2.88mb.

/D:DATE Tells the operating system to backup only those files that were last modified on or after the date specified. Thus you can use the command to be selective about the files that are copied. The date itself must be written in the format that is set by the COUNTRY.SYS in the CONFIG.SYS.

/T:TIME Allows you to backup only those files that have been modified or created on or after the specified time. You cannot use /T without also using /D.

[/L[:[DRIVE:] [PATH] LOGFILE]] This allows you to change the name of the default file that the command uses to store its information, i.e. the file normally called BACKUP.LOG. If you neglect to include the drive and path then the logfile will be placed in the root directory of the source directory. If you neglect to include a name for the logfile then the command will automatically use the name **BACKUP.LOG**.

141

BACKUP.EXE

Command Examples

1 To back-up an entire hard disk on Drive-A you would enter **BACKUP C:*.* A: /s**.

2 To back-up a specific directory to Drive-A you would enter **BACKUP C:\[DIRECTORY] *.* A:**.

3 To back-up only those files within a directory that have changed since August 28th. 1991 you would enter **BACKUP C:\[DIRECTORY] *.* A:/D:28-08-91**.

Error Messages

Entering the command by itself will produce the error message **No source drive specified**. You must use the command properly and specify a source and destination at the very least.

Notes

a. If you backup on to old backup disks then the program will automatically delete old files versions before writing the new ones. To prevent this use a /A parameter.

b. **BACKUP** does not make duplicates of the three main system files, i.e. IO.SYS, MSDOS.SYS and COMMAND.COM.

BACKUP.EXE

c. You cannot use **BACKUP** with any drive that has had **ASSIGN**, **JOIN** or **SUBST** applied to it.

d. **BACKUP** does not give you any indication of how many floppy disks that you will need to complete an operation.

e. **BACKUP** is one of those MS-DOS commands that can produce ERRORLEVEL codes which will have a different value depending on the result of the command's operation:

   0   BACKUP completed normally and correctly

   1   No files were found to backup hence operation aborted.

   2   Some of the files which should have been backed up were not due to a sharing conflict.

   3   The operation was terminated by a user before it was completed, e.g. by pressing Ctrl-C or Ctrl-Break.

   4   The operation was terminated due to an error not covered by the other codes.

BREAK

■ Operating System   ☐ Batch file   ■ Configuration

Description

Whenever the computer writes to the screen, gets input from the keyboard or sends a file to the printer, the operating system checks to see if you are pressing **Ctrl-C** or **Ctrl-Break**. This key combination means stops the current activity. You can force the operating system to check for the key combination more often, e.g. whenever it reads or writes to the disk, by adding this command to your CONFIG.SYS.

Command Syntax

BREAK=ON or **OFF**

Parameter Information

The command can be either On or Off. By default it is the latter. You may turn the command on or off from the system prompt if you prefer.

Command Examples

1. To turn the command on simply enter **BREAK=ON** at the system prompt. If you want the command to run all the time then you should add the two words to your CONFIG.SYS.

BREAK

Error Messages

There are no specific error messages for this command.

Notes

a. The one disadvantage of using this command is that it will slow down the operation of your system. The decrease in speed may be negligible but if you are doing something that involves a lot of disk activity, e.g. running Windows, then you may notice a definite speed decrease.

BUFFERS

☐ Operating System ☐ Batch file ■ Configuration

Description

Used to speed up disk access times by allocating some memory to hold data. The command is not vital as the operating system automatically assigns itself a number of buffers according to the computer system components. Each buffer is the same size as a single disk sector plus a small overhead.

Command Syntax

BUFFERS=N [,x]

Parameter Information

N You must set a number for the buffers if you use the command. The number can be in the range 1 to 99. However the operating system automatically assigns a number of buffers in accordance with the amount of RAM your system has:

BUFFERS=2 on a system with less than 128 Kb or RAM and fitted with a single low-density floppy disk.

BUFFERS=3 on a system fitted with less than 128 Kb of RAM but with disk capacity greater than 360 Kb.

BUFFERS=5 on a system with between 128 Kb and 255 Kb of RAM.

BUFFERS

BUFFERS=10 on any system with between 256 Kb and 511 Kb of RAM.

BUFFERS=15 on any system fitted with between 512 Kb and 640 Kb of memory.

,x Specifies the number of buffers in the secondary buffer cache. The value must be in the range 1 to 8 with 1 being the default. This secondary set of buffers is only of use if you are not using any other true disk program such as Microsoft SMARTDRV.

Command Examples

1   On a system with 640 Kb of RAM you would add a line saying **BUFFERS=15** in your CONFIG.SYS.

Error Messages

There are no specific error messages for this command.

Notes

a. Having too many buffers can be as bad as not having enough. Remember that each additional buffer uses a minimum of 532 Kb of memory. Therefore too many buffers is using memory that could be better used elsewhere.

147

BUFFERS

b. If you have loaded MS-DOS into the High Memory Area, i.e. by using **DOS=HIGH** in the CONFIG.SYS, then the buffers will also be in the HMA.

c. If you are using **SMARTDRV.SYS** then you can reduce the number of buffers to an absolute minimum, even omit them entirely, because Smartdrv is a true disk cache and so the **BUFFERS** become redundant.

CALL

☐ Operating System ■ Batch file ☐ Configuration

Description

Allows you to run one batch file from within another.

Command Syntax

CALL [DRIVE] [PATH] [BATCH FILE] [PARAMETERS]

Parameter Information

The parameters for this command are those for all batch files. For information on batch file parameters see the next chapter.

Command Examples

1   To call a batch file named BETA from within another batch file, called ALPHA, you would include the line CALL [DRIVE] [PATH] BETA into ALPHA.

Error Messages

There are no specific error messages for this command.

149

CALL

Notes

a. It is possible to call a batch file itself within the same batch file. For example you could have a batch file called BETA and include a line that says **CALL BETA** within that batch file. However if you do so you must allow some means whereby the call can be terminated and so return to the original.

CHCP

■ Operating System   ☐ Batch file   ☐ Configuration

Description

Allows you to see the currently set Active Code Page or change it.

Command Syntax

CHCP [NUMBER]

Parameter Information

The [NUMBER] must be one of the allowable code page values from the following list:

　　437 - USA. The default setting for all computers.
　　850 - Multilingual
　　852 - Slavic
　　860 - Portuguese
　　863 - French Canadian
　　865 - Nordic

Command Examples

1　To see what Active Code Page is currently set enter **CHCP** by itself.

CHCP

2   To change to another ACP simply enter **CHCP** followed by the appropriate number.

Error Messages

a. The only error message you are likely to encounter is **Invalid code page** when you use an incorrect number.

b. If a device cannot handle the changed code page you will get an error message saying **Code page [number] not prepared for device**.

Notes

a. I have never needed to set other code pages with this command.

CHDIR

■ Operating System   ☐ Batch file   ☐ Configuration

Description

Allows you to display the name and location of the current directory or change to another directory on the same disk. The command can be abbreviated to **CD**.

Command Syntax

CD [DIRECTORY]

Parameter Information

You may only change directory on the existing drive. There are so many possible ways to use this command that all examples of possible parameters are included below.

Command Examples

In all the following examples it is assumed that there are three sub-directories on your hard disk namely; C:\ALPHA, C:\ALPHA\BETA, C:\EPSILON, plus a directory named GAMMA on Drive-D.

1   **CD [directory]** allows you to move into a sub-directory of the current directory. For example, you can move from the root down into Alpha by entering **CD ALPHA** providing you are logged onto the root of Drive-C.

153

CHDIR

If you are logged onto Epsilon and enter **CD ALPHA** you will get an error message.

2   **CD** will take you directly back to the Root Directory of the current drive, e.g. from within C:\ALPHA\BETA or from C:\ALPHA or from C:\EPSILON if you enter **CD** you will go directly back to the root.

3   **CD\[directory]** allows you to move directly to another directory off the Root from within a sub-directory. For example you can move directly from Alpha to Epsilon by entering **CD\EPSILON** which takes you from Alpha up to the root and then down into Epsilon in one movement.

4   **CD..** simply takes you back up one level, i.e. to the parent of the current directory. From either Alpha or Epsilon this command will take you back to the root. If you are logged onto C:\ALPHA\BETA and you enter **CD..** then you will simply move up one level into C:\ALPHA.

5   **CD..\[directory]** takes you back up one level and down to the named directory which is on the same level as the current directory. In certain circumstances they can refer to the Root but it is more normal to allude to the Root using the backslash. A single dot,

CHDIR

which is displayed when using the **DIR** command, signifies the current directory.

6   Assume you are logged onto C:\ALPHA and you enter **CD D:\GAMMA**. Nothing apparently happens because the system prompt remains the same. By if you then log onto Drive-D by entering **D:** you will find that you are logged on to Gamma.

Error Messages

The main error message you will see with this command is **Invalid directory** which occurs when you try to log onto a directory that does not exist. It can also be caused because you omitted, or inadvertantly included, a backslash so that you are trying to go to a directory that does not exist.

CHKDSK.EXE

■ Operating System   ☐ Batch file   ☐ Configuration

Description

This command, which cannot be used on a network, is used to scan the disk and check the files for errors. Ideally, you want to run the program often, say once a week, to make sure that the disk is okay. Note, however, that **CHKDSK** does not normally check the actual disk, as you might think, instead it makes sure that both copies of the File Allocation Table match. The program can also be used to check files.

Command Syntax

CHKDSK [DRIVE][PATH] [FILENAME] [/F] [/V]

Parameter Information

[DRIVE] Must be a valid logical or physical drive and it must contain a disk.

[PATH] Specifies a specific subdirectory that you wish to check.

[FILENAME] The name of the file(s) you want checked.

[/F] Normally CHKDSK just notifies you of any errors but by including this parameter you can force the command to try and fix any errors it encounters.

CHKDSK.EXE

[/v] Forces the command to display the name of each file it encounters in the process of checking.

Command Examples

1. Enter **CHKDSK** without any parameters and the operating system will respond by checking the current disk and then displaying a report that looks something like this:

    Volume C   created 29 Mar 1990 1:14p
    Volume Serial Number is 1223-AB1F

    21282816 bytes total disk space
       98304 bytes in 6 hidden files
       40960 bytes in 18 directories
     8687616 bytes in 456 user files
    12455936 bytes available on disk

        2048 bytes in each allocation unit
       10392 total allocation units on disk
        6082 available allocation units on disk

      655360 bytes total memory
      307472 bytes free

2. Using the same disk but entering **CHKDSK/F** tells the command to try and fix any errors it finds. If there are any you will get a message saying something like:

157

CHKDSK.EXE

**5 lost allocation units found in 2 chains.
Convert lost chains to files (Y/N)?**

If you press **Y** then the chains will be assembled into files which are then placed in your root directory. Each file bears the name **FILE**NNNN**.CHK** where NNNN starts at 0001 and then runs consecutively. These files can then be deleted safely or dealt with in some other way.

If you press **N** then **CHKDSK** will fix the lost chains but not create files with them. The reason for doing so is that you cannot compress a disk that contains unattached chains.

Error Messages

There are no specific error messages for the command, only for what it finds.

Notes

a. **CHKDSK** will not work on any drive that is being operated on by the **ASSIGN, JOIN** or **SUBST** commands. Additionally, you should never run the command from within an application program that is using the disk at the same time.

b. The allocation units referred to are the clusters by which disk storage is allocated, in this case this particular disk is using a cluster size of 2 Kb.

CLS

■ Operating System   ■ Batch file   ☐ Configuration

Description

This command simply clears the screen. It can be very important in interactive batch files as a result.

Command Syntax

    CLS

Parameter Information

    There are no parameters for this command.

Command Examples

1   Enter **CLS** from the system prompt and the screen will clear. The cursor will then appear in the top left hand corner of the screen.

Error Messages

    There is no error message for this command.

COMMAND.COM

■ Operating System　　☐ Batch file　　☐ Configuration

Description

COMMAND.COM is the operating system interpreter. Without it the operating system will not work. COMMAND.COM is actually in two parts. The first component is always resident in the memory once the machine has been powered up and it is this part which provides the MS-DOS internal commands. The second portion is the 'transient' part. The various external commands are only loaded into the memory when they are needed and thereafter they are discarded. The advantage to this is that the entire system of commands does not have to be in the memory at any one time and thus you can run application programs that require a large part of the memory in order to function correctly. You can also use **COMMAND** as a command.

Command Syntax

COMMAND [DRIVE][PATH1] [DEVICE] [/E:X] [/P] [/C STRING] [/MSG]

Parameter Information

[DRIVE][PATH] Specifies the location of [DEVICE].

[DEVICE] The device to be used.

[/E:X] Sets the size for the environment in bytes. The value must be in the range 160 to 32768 in multiples of 16. The default value is 256.

COMMAND.COM

[/P] Makes the new copy of the command interpreter permanent and should only be used with the SHELL statement in the CONFIG.SYS.

[/C STRING] Specifies that the operating system is to perform the command specified in string and then stop.

[/MSG] Forces the operating system to store all error messages in memory. Useful only if you are running MS-DOS from a floppy disk. If you use this parameter you must also use /P.

Command Examples

1. **SHELL=C:\DOS\COMMAND.COM C:\DOS\/P** is the default that installing MS-DOS 5.0 will place into your CONFIG.SYS. In other words it installs COMMAND.COM as the permanent interpreter.

Error Messages

a. If you specify a value for /E that it incorrect you will get an error message saying **Parameter value not in allowed range**.

Notes

a. You can use any other device, e.g. CTTY, as a [DEVICE].

b. Running a second or subsequent command interpreter will use up memory.

161

COMP.EXE

■ Operating System ☐ Batch file ☐ Configuration

Description

COMP is used to compare the contents of two files or two groups of files. You can use the wildcards in place of actual filenames or have MS-DOS compare all the files in the specified sub-directories. You can also use the command without specifying anything, in which case MS-DOS will prompt you to supply the necessary information.

Command Syntax

COMP [DRIVE][PATH1][FILES1] [DRIVE][PATH2][FILES2] [/D] [/A] [/L] [/N=VALUE] [/C]

Parameter Information

[DRIVE] Must be a valid MS-DOS drive.

[PATH1] Specifies the locations of the first set of files.

[FILES1] The name of the first set of files to be compared. You may compare multiple files by using wildcards.

[PATH2] Specifies the location of the second set of files.

[FILES2] The name of the set of files to be compared with the first set.

COMP.EXE

[/D] Causes the difference in the files to be displayed in decimal format. By default differences are displayed in hex.

[/A] Displays file differences as characters.

[/L] Displays the number of lines on which differences are detected.

[/N=VALUE] Compares the number of lines in both files specified by VALUE rather than the entire file.

[/C] Makes the comparison between the files not case sensitive, i.e. alpha can be regarded as identical to ALPHA.

Command Examples

1 **COMP C:\SD1*.DOC D:\SD2*.DOC**. As the file comparison proceeds, the command will display the paths and filenames of the files being operated on. During the comparison itself the command will display a message detailing when there are mismatches within the files being compared, e.g.

   Compare error at OFFSET [value]
   file1 = [value]
   file2 = [value]

   The offset value and the values of the mismatches are given in Hexadecimal. If the command finds 10 mismatches it will automatically cancel with the message **10 Mismatches - ending compare**.

163

COMP.EXE

2   COMP C:\SD1*.DOC D:\SD2*.DOC /N=30. This allows you to compare files of different sizes - you can only do so by specifying the /N parameter. In this case the comparison will be the first 30 lines of each file. Should the files be of different sizes then MS-DOS tells you **Files are different sizes Compare more files (Y/N)?**. If you choose to continue then the command operates only until it reaches the end of the shorter of the two files. If the files contain no mismatches then the message **Files compare OK** appears.

Error Messages

There is no error message for this command as such, merely messages about the errors it finds.

Notes

a. If you are comparing a group of files they will be dealt with in pairs. After the first pair are checked the command automatically moves on to the next pair and so on. Once it reaches the end of the comparisons it will then ask **Compare more files (Y/N)?**. If you answer affirmatively then the command will prompt you to supply two new paths and/or filenames. If you answer negatively then the command terminates.

b. **COMP** compares files but if you want to compare entire disk contents then you are better off using **DISKCOMP**.

CONFIG.SYS

☐ Operating System ☐ Batch file ■ Configuration

Description

One of the two configuration files created by you to customise your system. The file is run as soon as COMMAND.COM has been loaded on start-up. The CONFIG.SYS may contain a range of device drivers and other customisation procedures.

Command Syntax

Not applicable.

Parameter Information

Not applicable.

Command Examples

    FILES=30
    BUFFERS=10
    LASTDRIVE=J
    DEVICE=C:\DOS\HIMEM.SYS
    DOS=HIGH,umb
    DEVICE=C:\DOS\EMM386.EXE NOEMS
    DEVICEHIGH=C:\DOS\RAMDRIVE.SYS 2560/E
    DEVICEHIGH=C:\DOS\SMARTDRV.SYS 1024 512
    DEVICEHIGH=C:\DOS\SETVER.EXE
    COUNTRY=044,,C:\DOS\COUNTRY.SYS

CONFIG.SYS

Error Messages

Not applicable. Any error message will be caused by a line in the file bearing an error. As the computer boots up you will get a message saying **Error in CONFIG.SYS line x** followed by a possible cause of the error.

Notes

a. See the preceding chapter for more details about this file.

COPY

■ Operating System   ☐ Batch file   ☐ Configuration

Description

COPY allows you to make duplicate copies of files to another location. You can also use the command to copy an input from the keyboard directly into a file.

Command Syntax

COPY [SOURCE] [FILENAME(S)] [DESTINATION] [FILENAME(S)] [/A or /B] [/V]

Parameter Information

[SOURCE] The directory, and where necessary a path, that contains the files you want copied.

[FILENAME(S)] The file or group of files to be copied. You may use wildcards to copy groups of files.

[DESTINATION] The target to which the file(s) are to be copied.

[/A] Specifies that the files to be copied are ASCII files. The parameter may be either before or after the filenames. If it is before it applies to all files that follow it until you change to using the parameter below.

167

COPY

[/B] Specifies that the file being copied are binary files. It may appear before or after the filenames and applies to all files until the parameter above is used.

[/V] Forces the command to verify every copy process to ensure the file(s) are written correctly to disk.

Command Examples

1. To copy all files from C:\ALPHA to C:\BETA, enter **COPY C:\ALPHA*.* C:\BETA**.

2. To copy only those files that have an extension of .DOC from the same source to the same target enter **COPY C:\ALPHA*.DOC C:\BETA**.

3. To make duplicate copies of files but change their extension you can enter **COPY *.DOC *.TXT**. This will copy every file with an extension of .DOC and make duplicate files, each bearing the same filename, but each will have the extension of .TXT. You can combine this version of the command with the previous one by entering **COPY *.DOC C:\BETA*.DOC** which will copy the files into C:\BETA but also change their extensions at the same time.

COPY

4 To copy whatever you type from the keyboard into an ASCII file, e.g. the CONFIG.SYS, enter **COPY CON [FILENAME]**. The acronym CON refers to the keyboard and anything you type will be stored in memory until you press **F6** or **Ctrl-Z** when the data will then be written to the designated filename.

5 You can also use the command to concatenate files, i.e. join two or more files together into one, by entering **COPY [FILENAME1]+[FILENAME2] [FILENAME3]**, where [FILENAME1] and [FILENAME2] are the two files to be joined and [FILENAME3] is the name for the joined file. Note you cannot use the same filename for either of the first two files and for the destination file. If you do so the original file will be overwritten before it can be concatenated and so the process stops.

You can also use wildcards with this use of the command by entering **COPY *.TXT [FILENAME]**. In which case every file with an extension of .TXT will be concatenated into a single file. The original files will also remain in place on the disk.

6 You can print pure ASCII files by sending them directly to the printer by entering **COPY [FILENAME] PRN**.

169

COPY

Error Messages

a. If you try to concatenate two files and then use the filename of one of them for the destination file you will get an error message saying **Content of destination lost before copy**.

b. If you try to copy a file within the same directory or drive to the same filename you get an error message saying **File cannot be copied to itself 0 File(s) copied**.

c. If you mis-spell a filename or ask for a non-existent one then you get the error message **File not found - [filename] 0 File(s) copied**.

Notes

a. **COPY** cannot be used for copying sub-directories, it can only be used for files.

COUNTRY.SYS

☐ Operating System ☐ Batch file ■ Configuration

Description

Allows you to set national characteristics for the computer system. By default all computers operate as American but by using this device in the CONFIG.SYS you can customise certain national operands.

Command Syntax

COUNTRY=[COUNTRY CODE VALUE],[CODE PAGE],[DRIVE][PATH] COUNTRY.SYS

Parameter Information

[COUNTRY CODE VALUE] Must be one of the valid country codes. See below.

[CODE PAGE] Specifies the code page for the country.

[DRIVE][PATH] The location of the COUNTRY.SYS file.

Command Examples

1 The following is the normal setting for using a computer in the UK, assuming that your MS-DOS files are stored on Drive-C in a directory called DOS:
   COUNTRY=044,,C:\DOS\COUNTRY.SYS.

COUNTRY.SYS

Error Messages

The major error message you will see is **Invalid country code or code page** when you use an incorrect value.

Notes

a. There are a huge range of possible country codes which affect the display of the date and time amongst other things, that can be applied to this command. The full list is:

Country	Code	Code Pages	Date Format
Belgium	032	850,437	dd/mm/yy
Brazil	055	850,437	dd/mm/yy
Canadian-French	002	863,850	yy/mm/dd
Czechoslovakia	042	852,850	yy-mm-dd
Denmark	045	850,865	dd-mm-yy
Finland	358	850,437	dd.mm.yy
France	033	850,437	dd.mm.yy
Germany	049	850,437	dd.mm.yy
Hungary	036	852,850	yy-mm-dd
International English	061	437,850	dd/mm/yy
Italy	039	850,437	dd/mm/yy
Latin America	003	850,437	dd/mm/yy
Netherlands	031	850,437	dd-mm-yy
Norway	047	850,865	dd.mm.yy
Poland	048	852,850	yy-mm-dd
Portugal	351	850,860	dd-mm-yy
Spain	034	850,437	dd/mm/yy
Sweden	046	850,437	yy-mm-dd
Switzerland	041	850,437	dd.mm.yy

COUNTRY.SYS

Country	Code	Code Pages	Date Format
U.K.	044	437,850	dd/mm/yy
United States	001	437,850	mm/dd/yy
Yugoslavia	038	852,850	yy-mm-dd

b. There are special versions of MS-DOS with their own code pages for Arabic, Israel, Japan, Korea, People's Republic of China, and Taiwan.

CTTY

■ Operating System　　☐ Batch file　　☐ Configuration

Description

Changes the terminal device used by the computer system. For example, you can have the main input device of the machine being what comes in over the COM ports rather than via the keyboard.

Command Syntax

CTTY [DEVICE]

Parameter Information

[DEVICE] This can be any of the valid alternative devices i.e. PRN, LPT1, LPT2, LPT3, CON, AUX, COM1, COM2, COM3 or COM4.

Command Examples

1　　To have the main input device being COM1 you would enter **CTTY COM1**. To switch back to the keyboard you would then input **CTTY CON** from the remote device.

Error Messages

The main error message you will see is **Invalid device**.

CTTY

Notes

a. If you use this command without having a remote device connected you may well find that the only way to get your machine back to normal is to reboot it completely.

b. Unless you are using an alternative device as a matter of course, you should never include this command in your CONFIG.SYS.

DATE

■ Operating System   ☐ Batch file   ■ Configuration

Description

Allows you to change the current date on the computer system.

Command Syntax

> **DATE**

Parameter Information

> There are no parameters for this command.

Command Examples

> 1   Enter **DATE** at the system prompt and the computer responds with
>
>   **Current date is Thu 29/08/1991**
>   **Enter new date (dd-mm-yy):**
>
>   You simply enter the new date, following the syntax shown, and this will be written into the computer BIOS for you.

DATE

Error Messages

The only error message you will see is **Invalid date** caused by entering the date in the wrong order or using the incorrect dividers, e.g. you have used a hyphen instead of a forward slash.

Notes

a. If you do not have an AUTOEXEC.BAT then you will be asked to change the date every time that computer boots up. By just pressing **Enter** you accept the current settings.

DEBUG.EXE

■ Operating System ☐ Batch file ☐ Configuration

Description

DEBUG is used for testing and debugging executable files.

Command Syntax

> **DEBUG** [DRIVE][PATH] FILENAME [PARAMETERS]

Parameter Information

> [DRIVE][PATH] Specifies the location of FILENAME.

> **DEBUG** probably has more parameters than any other MS-DOS command. This is due to the fact that it is really a fully fledged program in its own right. The possible parameters are:

> **?** Displays a list of the possible DEBUG commands.

> **A** [ADDRESS] Assembles 8086, 8087 and 8088 mnemonics from the stated address.

> **C** [RANGE] Compares two selections.

> **D** [LOCATION] Shows the contents of a memory location.

> **E** [VALUE] Enters data into memory locations starting at the specified address.

DEBUG.EXE

F [RANGE VALUES] Fills the range with specified values.

G [ADDRESS] Runs the program file that is located at the address.

H [VALUE1 VALUE2] Calculates the arithmetic associated with the two values - in hexadecimal.

I [PORT] Shows a one byte value from the specified port.

L [ADDRESS] [DRIVE] [SECTOR] [VALUE] Loads the contents of the a file or disk sector into memory.

M [RANGE] [ADDRESS] Copies the contents of a block of memory to another address.

N [PATH] Specifies the location of a file for use with the L or W command.

O [PORT] [VALUE] Sends the specified value to the nominated port.

P [ADDRESS] [VALUE] Executes a sub-routine from the specified address.

Q Quit and return to the system prompt.

R [REGISTER] Displays the contents of a register or changes it.

S [RANGE] [LIST] Searches the specified addresses for the value in list.

DEBUG.EXE

T [ADDRESS] [VALUE] Executes an instruction and then displays the values of all registers.

U [RANGE] Unassembles the program from range.

W [ADDRESS] [DRIVE] [SECTOR] [NUMBER] Writes the file being tested to the disk starting at the specified sector.

XA Allocates expanded memory.

XD Frees expanded memory.

XM Maps expanded memory.

XS Shows the status of expanded memory.

Command Examples

DEBUG is not a program for which examples can be included. It is intended for those people who are au fait with more than just the basics of computers and as such it is outside the scope of this book.

Error Messages

See a detailed book about this program for these.

DEL

■ Operating System   ☐ Batch file   ☐ Configuration

Description

DEL allows you to delete files from any drive or sub-directory.

Command Syntax

> **DEL** [DRIVE][PATH] [FILENAME(S)] /P

Parameter Information

> [DRIVE][PATH] Specifies the location of the filenames to be erased.
>
> /P Provides for you to confirm each deletion before it occurs.

Command Examples

1. To delete all files in the current directory with the extension of .TXT enter **DEL *.TXT**.

2. To delete all the files in the current directory starting with the letter A enter **DEL A*.***.

3. To delete every file in a directory enter **DEL *.*** or move up one level in the directory structure and then

181

DEL

enter **DEL [DIRECTORY]**. The operating system will respond with a message saying:

**All files in directory will be deleted!
Are you sure (Y/N)?**

If you answer affirmatively, by pressing **Y**, then the files will be deleted. If you press **N** then the command terminates without further action.

Error Messages

There are no error messages other than **File not found**.

Notes

a. When files are deleted they are not actually removed from your disk or overwritten. Instead the first character of the filename is changed to the Greek character Sigma. This tells the operating system that it can use the space formerly occupied by that file for writing new files to. You can recover erased files by using a utility because this allows you to change Sigma, which you will not actually be shown, back to a standard character and so 'resurrect' the file. MS-DOS now includes a command called **UNDELETE** to allow you to do this.

b. **DEL** does not erase directories - you must use the **RMDIR** command instead.

DELOLDOS.EXE

■ Operating System   ☐ Batch file   ☐ Configuration

Description

The purpose of this command is to remove the copy of the old operating system that was created when you installed MS-DOS 5.0.

Command Syntax

DELOLDOS [/B]

Parameter Information

[/B] Uses monochrome instead of the default colour display.

Command Examples

1   **DELOLDOS** will bring up a large, full screen, message giving you the option of removing all old MS-DOS files from your hard disk. Press **Y** will allow the command to proceed. Pressing **N** terminates it. Thereafter all the old file will be erased followed by DELOLDOS itself.

Error Messages

There is no error message for this command.

DEVICE

☐ Operating System ☐ Batch file ■ Configuration

Description

DEVICE, which must be in the CONFIG.SYS, allows you to install various device drivers for configuring the system.

Command Syntax

DEVICE=[DRIVE][PATH] [DEVICE] [DEVICE PARAMETERS] which will load the device into the low memory area,

or

DEVICEHIGH=[DRIVE][PATH] [DEVICE] [DEVICE PARAMETERS] to load a device into the High Memory Area.

Parameter Information

[DRIVE][PATH] Specifies the location of the device you want to install.

[DEVICE] Any of the available device drivers.

[DEVICE PARAMETERS] Those parameters that apply to the specific device you wish to install.

DEVICE

Command Examples

1   To install a Ramdrive you would include a line in your CONFIG.SYS saying:

DEVICE=C:\DOS\RAMDRIVE.SYS 2560 /E

This creates a ramdrive of 2.5 Mb which uses extended memory.

Error Messages

a. An incorrect use of a device will cause an error message specific to that device to appear.

b. If the device file is not at the specified location then an error message saying **File not found** will appear.

Notes

a. The full range of installable devices supplied with MS-DOS 5.0 include ANSI.SYS, DISPLAY.SYS, DRIVER.SYS, EGA.SYS, EMM386.EXE, HIMEM.SYS, PRINTER.SYS, RAMDRIVE.SYS and SMARTDRV.SYS. Each of these is covered separately within this chapter.

b. HIMEM.SYS and EMM386.EXE cannot be loaded into the High Memory Area.

DEVICE

c. In order to use the High Memory Area you must include a line saying **DOS=HIGH,UMB** within the CONFIG.SYS before any lien that tries to load device drivers other than those mentioned in (b) above.

d. If you omit the **DOS=HIGH,UMB** line or leave off the **,UMB** then all devices will be loaded into the Conventional Memory Area.

e. If you try to load a device into the HMA and there is insufficient room your system may lock up. Use the Emergency Boot Disk to boot your system and then correct the error. Load the offending device into conventional memory to find out how much space it needs.

DIR

■ Operating System ☐ Batch file ☐ Configuration

Description

Used to display a list of files and/or directories in any directory or on any drive. This command is one that has been radically updated since the last release of MS-DOS and now includes a large range of possible parameters.

Command Syntax

DIR [DRIVE][PATH] [FILESPEC] [/W] [/P] [/A:ATTRIBUTES] [/O:ORDER] [/S] [/B] [/L]

Parameter Information

[DRIVE][PATH] Specifies the location of the directory and/or the files to be displayed.

[FILESPEC] Any use of wildcards or filename you may be looking for.

[/W] Displays the file listing in five columns across the screen and as a result does not show the file sizes or time and date information.

[/P] Displays the file listing in blocks of 23 with the message **Press any key to continue...** at the bottom of the screen. Pressing any key then displays the next block of up to 23 files. The message will appear if there are more to be displayed.

DIR

[/A:ATTRIBUTES] Causes the display to be only of those files, and sub-directories, which have attributes that match those specified. You may use multiple attributes in combination. The possible attributes are:

- **H**   Hidden files.
- **-H** Not hidden files.
- **S**   System files.
- **-S** Non-system files.
- **D**   Directories
- **-D** Display only files.
- **A**   Files with the Archive attribute set to on.
- **-A** Files with the Archive attribute set to off.
- **R**   Files which are Read-Only.
- **-R** Files that are not Read-Only.

[/O:ORDER] Forces the display to match the order that you specify. You may use multiple parameters in combination. The possible order parameters are:

- **D**   By date order, earliest first.
- **-D** Reverse date order, youngest first.
- **E**   In alphabetical order based on the extension name.
- **-E** In reverse order based on extension names.
- **G**   With directories appearing before files.
- **-G** With files listed before directories.
- **N**   In alphabetical order based on filenames, A to Z.
- **-N** In reverse alphabetical order, i.e. Z to A.
- **S**   In order of size, smallest first.
- **-S** Reverse size order, i.e. largest first.

DIR

[/s] Displays every occurrence of the specified filename in all sub-directories subtended off the specified directory.

[/B] Produces a display as if no parameters were used but does not give file size or the time and date information. Cannot be used with the /w parameter.

[/L] Displays the files and/or directories in lower case.

Command Examples

1   To display the files in a directory in order of their extension in five columns you would enter **DIR /OE/W**. Files with no extensions will appear first.

2   To display only those files beginning with the letter A you would enter **DIR A*.***.

3   To display the files in C:\ALPHA from the root directory you need to enter the full path, e.g. **DIR C:\ALPHA**. You can add any of the parameters to this if you wish.

4   You can combine sort orders in which case the files are sorted in the order that you place the orders. For example, entering **DIR /O-ES** will display the files in reverse order based on the extensions with the smallest files appearing in any alphabetic group first. Entering

DIR

DIR /os-e give a different display because the sort order is different.

Error Messages

The main error message that will appear is **Parameter format not correct - [character]** where the character is incorrect.

Notes

a. The different ways of displaying files with this command may take you some time to get used to.

DIRCMD

☐ Operating System   ☐ Batch file   ■ Configuration

Description

You can use this command to preset the appearance of the file list when you use the **DIR** command. The command line has to be included in the AUTOEXEC.BAT. You can override this by using any parameter with **DIR**.

Command Syntax

SET DIRCMD=[PARAMETER]

Parameter Information

The parameter(s) can be any of the valid **DIR** parameters.

Command Examples

1   **SET DIRCMD**=/w means that whenever you enter **DIR** the files are automatically displayed in the five column format.

Error Messages

The only error message you are likely to encounter will be **Invalid parameter - ?** where **?** is the illegal character.

DISKCOMP.COM

■ Operating System   ☐ Batch file   ☐ Configuration

Description

DISKCOMP allows you to compare two floppy disks to check a duplication. It does more than just check that each disk contains the same files, instead it checks the disk itself to make sure that the sectors on each disk are identical.

Command Syntax

DISKCOMP [DRIVE1] [DRIVE2] [/1] [/8]

Parameter Information

[DRIVE1] This is the first drive that contains one of the disks to be checked.

[DRIVE2] Is the second drive.

[/1] Forces the command to only check the first side of a disk.

[/8] Forces the command to check only the first 8 sectors of each track regardless of how many sectors the tracks actually contain.

DISKCOMP.COM

Command Examples

1. To compare two disks in different drives enter **DISKCOMP A: B:**.

2. To compare two disks in a machine with only one drive you can enter **DISKCOMP A: A:**. You will then be prompted to swop disks as necessary. Alternatively you can just enter **DISKCOMP A:** which has the same effect.

Error Messages

The error messages you get from this command depend on what it finds when it compares the two disks.

a. **Invalid drive specification Specified drive does not exist or is non-removable** is the message that appears if you try to use the command on hard disks.

b. If the disks are identical you get a message saying **Compare OK Compare another diskette (Y/N)?**. Pressing **Y** allows you to compare two more disks, pressing **N** terminates the command.

c. If the disks are not identical you will get a message saying **Compare error on side x, track y**.

d. You may get a message saying **Compare error on side 0, track 0** if you are comparing two disks and one of them is a duplicate of the other created with the COPY command - even

DISKCOMP.COM

though both disks contain the same data. This is because the data may not be in the same sectors.

Notes

a. DISKCOMP only works with floppy disks - you cannot use it to compare hard disks, either physical or logical ones.

b. You cannot use **DISKCOMP** on a network or any drive that is used with **ASSIGN, JOIN** or **SUBST**.

c. **DISKCOMP** produces errorlevel codes:

    0 The disks are identical.

    1 The disks are not identical.

    2 Operation terminated by pressing Ctrl-C or Ctrl-Break.

    3 A hardware fault occurred.

    4 An initialisation error occurred.

DISKCOPY.COM

■ Operating System   ☐ Batch file   ☐ Configuration

Description

DISKCOPY is used to create identical copies of a floppy disk. The disks must be of the same size, capacity and type. The second disk need not be pre-formatted. Any data on the second disk will be destroyed as the process takes place.

Command Syntax

DISKCOPY [DRIVE1] [DRIVE2] [/1] [/v]

Parameter Information

[DRIVE1] This is the first drive that contains one of the disks to be copied. The size, capacity and type of disk in this drive determines what the second disk must be.

[DRIVE2] Is the second drive.

[/1] Forces the command to only copy the first side of a disk.

[/v] Forces the command to verify the copying process.

Command Examples

1. Provided you have two floppy drives of the same size and type you can enter **DISKCOPY A: B:**.

DISKCOPY.COM

2. If you do not have two drives of the same size and type you can enter **DISKCOPY A: A:** which will use only one drive. You will be prompted to switch disks as necessary.

Error Messages

a. **Invalid drive specification Specified drive does not exist or is non-removable** is the message that appears if you try to use the command on hard disks.

b. Once the copy is completed the command displays **Copy another diskette (Y/N)?**. Press **Y** to do so or **N** to terminate the command.

c. If you are copying to an unformatted disk then you will get a message saying **Formatting while copying**.

d. If the source disk is larger than the target disk then you will get a message saying **TARGET media has lower capacity than SOURCE Continue anyway (Y/N)?**. Press **Y** to do so, **N** to terminate the command. If you do continue **DISKCOPY** will try to format the target disk but this may be unsuccessful.

Notes

a. You cannot use **DISKCOPY** with a hard disk.

b. Because the command produces an exact copy of the original any errors, faults or problems will also occur on the copy.

DISKCOPY.COM

c. **DISKCOPY** produces errorlevel codes:

   0 The copy was successful.

   1 A non-fatal error occurred.

   2 Operation terminated by pressing Ctrl-C or Ctrl-Break.

   3 A hardware fault occurred.

   4 An initialisation error occurred.

DISPLAY.SYS

☐ Operating System   ☐ Batch file   ■ Configuration

Description

This device driver allows you to switch the code pages for the console. It must be installed in the CONFIG.SYS.

Command Syntax

> **DEVICE=**[DRIVE][PATH] **DISPLAY.SYS CON :=(**[TYPE],[CODE PAGE],[N] [,M]**)**

Parameter Information

[DRIVE][PATH] Specifies the location of DISPLAY.SYS.

[TYPE] The display adaptor that is fitted to your system. Valid types are CGA, EGA, LCD and MONO. If you omit this then the command checks your system to decide what display adaptor is in use.

[CODE PAGE] Any of the valid code page values. Possible values are:

- **437** United States of America
- **850** Latin 1 - Multilingual
- **852** Slavic - Latin II
- **860** Portuguese
- **863** Canadian-French
- **865** Nordic

DISPLAY.SYS

[N] Specifies the total number of code pages that the device can support in addition to the first page specified in the previous parameter. Values can be in the range of 0 to 6. The actual value depends on your hardware.

[M] Specifies the number of fonts the hardware can support.

Command Examples

1 To set the display for a UK system with a VGA monitor you would include the line **DEVICE= C:\DOS\DISPLAY.SYS** CON:=(EGA,437).

   Note that EGA applies to both EGA monitors and VGA or even SVGA ones. The code page is the same as for the USA because there is no specific code page for the UK.

Error Messages

The only associated error messages refer to location or grammatical errors.

Notes

a. If you are using any third party display driver this must be installed before DISPLAY.SYS to avoid any possibility of corruption.

DOS

☐ Operating System　　☐ Batch file　　■ Configuration

Description

Allows you to relocate MS-DOS into the High Memory Area and maintain links between the conventional memory area and the high memory area.

Command Syntax

DOS=[HIGH or LOW][,UMB or NOUMB]

Parameter Information

[HIGH] Places DOS into the HMA.

[LOW] Places DOS into conventional memory. This is the default and if you omit this command entirely then DOS is placed into the conventional memory area.

[,UMB] Provides a link between the high memory area and the conventional memory area. If you do not have this parameter then you cannot place devices into the high memory area.

[,NOUMB] Disconnects the link between the two memory areas.

DOS

Command Examples

1   **DOS**=HIGH,UMB places DOS into the High Memory Area and allows you to place other device drivers into the same area.

Error Messages

There are no error messages other than grammatical ones.

Notes

a. To use the High Memory Area you must have a minimum of 1 Mb of RAM fitted to your machine - preferably more.

DOSKEY.COM

■ Operating System　　☐ Batch file　　☐ Configuration

Description

This is a totally new command for MS-DOS. At its simplest it allows you to recall commands. It will also allows you to edit command lines and create macros.

Command Syntax

>   DOSKEY [/REINSTALL] [/BUFSIZE=VALUE] [/MACROS] [/HISTORY] [/INSERT] [/OVERSTRIKE] [MACRONAME[=NAME]]

Parameter Information

>   [/REINSTALL] Does just that, it reinstalls the program and clears all existing buffers.

>   [/BUFSIZE=VALUE] Specifies a size for the buffer in which commands lines are stored. By default the value is 512 bytes. The minimum size is 256 bytes.

>   [/MACROS] Displays a list of existing macros. Note, MS-DOS does not include any sample macros. This parameter may be abbreviated to /M.

>   [/HISTORY] Gives you list of all the command lines that are stored in the memory, e.g. those commands that have been issued since DOSKEY was installed. The command lines are stored on the basis of first in, first out.

DOSKEY.COM

[/INSERT] Turns off insert mode.

[/OVERSTRIKE] Turns on overstrike mode.

[MACRONAME[=NAME]] The first part specifies a name you want to use for a macro. The second part defines a list of commands you want to include.

Command Examples

1. **DOSKEY** entered from the system prompt loads the command into memory and makes its simplest functions available. See below for command keys.

Error Messages

There are no error messages for the simple version of DOSKEY.

Notes

a. Once you have loaded **DOSKEY** you can use the following keys to recall commands:

   Up Displays the last command used.

   Dn Displays the next command in the list or returns you to the prompt.

   PgUp Displays the first command available in the buffer.

DOSKEY.COM

PgDn Displays the last command in the buffer.

Right Moves the cursor right one character.

Left Moves the cursor left one character.

Ctrl-Left Move the cursor to the start of the previous word.

Ctrl-Right Moves the cursor to the start of the following word.

Home Moves the cursor to the start of the line.

End Moves the cursor to the end of the line.

Esc Clears the displayed command line from the screen but leaves it in the buffer.

F1 Copies the last command from the buffer to the screen one character at a time.

F2 LETTER Searches through the command string for the letter you press after the function key. If the letter does not exist then nothing happens.

F3 Copies the rest of the command line from the current cursor position.

F4 ? Deletes characters from the cursor position up to the letter, which replaces the question mark, you press.

F5 Copies the displayed command line to the buffer but does not execute it.

DOSKEY.COM

F6 Places an end of file marker (Ctrl-Z) at the end of the command line.

F7 Displays all the commands that are stored in the memory, each preceded by a number showing the order they were placed into the buffer.

F8 Allows you to do a specific search for commands. Type the first few letters of the command you want and then press **F8**. **DOSKEY** does the rest and displays the first matching command that it finds in the buffer.

F9 Allows you to select a command by number. It helps if you press **F7** first so you can see which number you want.

Alt-F7 Deletes all the commands from the buffers.

Alt-F10 Deletes all macros from the buffers.

DOSSHELL.COM

■ Operating System   ☐ Batch file   ☐ Configuration

Description

If you don't like the system prompt and do not have Windows you can use **DOSSHELL** as a graphical user interface for MS-DOS. DOSSHELL is not so much a command as a program.

Command Syntax

DOSSHELL [/T or /G] [:RES[N]] [/B]

Parameter Information

[/T] Starts the DOSSHELL program in text mode.

[/G] Starts the program in graphic mode.

[:RES] Specifies a resolution for the monitor. You may use L for low, M for medium or H for high.

[N] Specifies a second screen resolution.

[/B] Starts the program in monochrome mode.

Command Examples

1. To start the shell program in graphic mode enter **DOSSHELL**/G. This gives you little icons and text.

DOSSHELL.COM

2. To use text mode enter **DOSSHELL**/T which gives you text but no icons.

Error Messages

Any error message that occurs will be due to misuse of other commands within the program.

Notes

a. **DOSSWAP.EXE** is a sub-program of **DOSSHELL** and cannot be run by itself.

b. For details of using **DOSSHELL** see the Appendices.

DRIVER.SYS

☐ Operating System ☐ Batch file ■ Configuration

Description

This is a device driver which must be installed via the CONFIG.SYS. Its purpose to create a logical drive that can be dealt with as if it was a physical drive.

Command Syntax

DEVICE=[DRIVE][PATH] **DRIVER.SYS** /D:VALUE [/C] [/F:TYPE] [/H:HEADS] [/S:SECTORS] [/T:TRACKS]

Parameter Information

[DRIVE][PATH] Specifies the location of DRIVER.SYS.

/D:VALUE Specifies the number of the physical floppy disk drive. The number must be in the range 0 to 127. Drive-A, the first physical drive, is **0**, Drive-B is **1** and so on.

[/c] Tells the operating system that the disk drive can tell when its catch is closed or not, i.e. when there is a disk in place.

[/F:TYPE] Specifies the type of disk drive where TYPE is a number. If you use this parameter you can omit any of the following ones. Possible values for type are:

0 - 160 Kb, 180 Kb, 320 Kb or 360 Kb drives.
1 - 1.2 Mb 5.25" drive.

DRIVER.SYS

    2 - 720 Kb 3.5" disks. (The default type.)

    7 - 1.44 Mb 3.5" drive.

    9 - 2.88 Mb 3.5" disks.

[/H:HEADS] Specifies the number of heads in the drive. Values range between 1 and 99.

[/S:SECTORS] Specifies the number of sectors for the disk in the range 1 to 99.

[/T:TRACKS] Specifies the number of tracks in the range 1 to 999.

Command Examples

    1   **DEVICE=C:\DOS\DRIVER.SYS /D:2**

Error Messages

The main error that will occur will be grammatical due to the fact of entering invalid values.

DRIVPARM

☐ Operating System ☐ Batch file ■ Configuration

Description

Defines or modifies the parameters for block devices, e.g. drives, of any existing physical drive. The command must be placed in the CONFIG.SYS.

Command Syntax

DRIVPARM=/D:VALUE [/C] [/F:TYPE] [/H:HEADS] [/I] [/N] [/S:SECTORS] [/T:TRACKS]

Parameter Information

/D:VALUE Specifies the number of the physical floppy disk drive. The number must be in the range 0 to 127. Drive-A, the first physical drive, is **0**, Drive-B is **1** and so on.

[/C] Tells the operating system that the disk drive in question can tell when its catch is closed or not.

[/F:TYPE] Specifies the type of disk drive where TYPE is a number. If you use this parameter you can omit any of the following ones. Possible values for type are:

  0 - 160 Kb, 180 Kb, 320 Kb or 360 Kb drives.
  1 - 1.2 Mb 5.25" drive.
  2 - 720 Kb 3.5" disks. (The default type.)
  5 - Hard disk

DRIVPARM

6 - Tape
7 - 1.44 Mb 3.5" drive.
8 - Read/Write Optical Disk.
9 - 2.88 Mb 3.5" disks.

[/H:HEADS] Specifies the number of heads in the drive. Values range between 1 and 99.

[/I] Specifies that the drive in question is using the same controller as that used by existing disk drives.

[/N] Specifies a non-removable device.

[/S:SECTORS] Specifies the number of sectors for the disk in the range 1 to 99.

[/T:TRACKS] Specifies the number of tracks in the range 1 to 999.

Command Examples

DRIVPARM=/D:2

Error Messages

The main error that will occur will be grammatical due to the fact of entering invalid values.

ECHO

☐ Operating System　　■ Batch file　　☐ Configuration

Description

Turns on and off the display of commands or can be used to display a message on screen. When you run a batch file, the commands it contains can be displayed on screen if you turn this feature on, or they can be not displayed if you turn it off.

Command Syntax

[@] ECHO [ON or OFF] [MESSAGE]

Parameter Information

[@] Because **ECHO** is in itself a command it will appear on screen. You can stop this happening by preceded it with the @ sign.

[ON] Turns the display feature on.

[OFF] Turn the display feature off.

[MESSAGE] Can be any string of text you wish.

Command Examples

1   To display a message on screen you would have a line in the batch file saying, for example, **ECHO This**

ECHO

is a line of text. The words in bold will appear on screen exactly as they are typed. You can only have a maximum of 60 characters in a line. If you need several lines of text to appear on screen you need to have several ECHO statements for them.

2   To turn the echoing facility off you would have a line in the batch file saying **ECHO** OFF. However, this will cause the command line itself to appear on screen so you are better off having **@ECHO** OFF which means that this line will not appear on screen.

Error Messages

You are unlikely to get any error messages with this command because it is difficult to mis-spell the word. However, you will have to check the text in any message carefully because it will appear exactly as you type it.

Notes

a. ECHO really comes into its own when you create interactive batch files.

213

EDIT.COM

■ Operating System   ☐ Batch file   ☐ Configuration

Description

EDIT is a full screen editor - something that every person who uses MS-DOS has wanted for a long time! The program can only be used with pure ASCII files but it will allow you to load, save, print and modify any text file. It is really part of QBASIC and if you delete this from the disk you cannot use the editor.

Command Syntax

EDIT [DRIVE][PATH] [FILENAME] [/B] [/G] [/H] [NOHI]

Parameter Information

[DRIVE][PATH] Specifies the location of a file that you want to load and edit.

[FILENAME] The name of the pure ASCII file that you want to load or create. If you specify a name that does not exist then **EDIT** will still start and it automatically creates the file for you.

[/B] Forces the command to use monochrome mode.

[/G] Uses fast screen updating on CGA monitors.

[/H] Forces the command to use the maximum number of lines possible on the monitor type you are using.

EDIT.COM

[/NOHI] Allows you to use a maximum of 8 colours for the editor. Normally it will try to use 16 colours.

Command Examples

1	**EDIT AUTOEXEC.BAT** will start the text editor and load the AUTOEXEC file for you.

Error Messages

There are no error messages that this command can generate.

Notes

a. See the previous chapter for more examples of using the text editor.

b. The available commands in the text editor are also covered in the Appendices.

EDLIN.EXE

■ Operating System   ☐ Batch file   ☐ Configuration

Description

EDLIN is the old text editor that came with all previous versions of MS-DOS. It operates on the basis of lines and when compared to EDIT (See previous section) one wonders why it is included.

Command Syntax

EDLIN [DRIVE][PATH] [FILENAME] [/B]

Parameter Information

[DRIVE][PATH] Specifies the location of the file you want to load and modify or create.

[/B] Allows the program to ignore end of file characters.

Command Examples

1   **EDLIN C:\AUTOEXEC.BAT** will load the named file ready for editing.

Error Messages

a. None within the program though any changes you make may cause their own errors when the file is run.

EDLIN.EXE

Notes

EDLIN comes complete with a range of control codes which are:

[LINE] Displays the line specified. The line must be a valid one, i.e. within the actual number of lines of the file being edited.

? Displays a list of the **EDLIN** control codes.

[N] A Loads a piece of the file into memory. [N] specifies the number of lines to be so loaded.

[LINE1],[LINE2],[LINE3],[COUNT] C Copies a block of lines into memory. Where [LINE1] specifies the first line number; [LINE2] specifies the last line number; [LINE3] specifies the line number before which the block is to be inserted; [COUNT] specifies the number of times the block is to be inserted.

[LINE1],[LINE2] D Deletes a block of consecutive lines. [LINE1] specifies the first line to be deleted. [LINE2] specifies the last line of a block to be deleted. All the lines between the two will be erased.

E Saves the file to disk and terminates **EDLIN**.

[LINE] I Inserts lines before the line number specified.

[LINE1],[LINE2] L Lists the block of lines between the two numbers specified.

[LINE1],[LINE2],LINE3 M Move the specified block of lines to another location.

EDLIN.EXE

[LINE1],[LINE2] P Displays the block of lines in the range specified.

Q Terminates EDLIN without saving the loaded file to disk.

[LINE1],[LINE2] [?] R [STRING1] Ctrl-Z [STRING2] Searches for every occurrence of the string of characters specified in [STRING1] and replaces it with the text in [STRING2]. The question mark forces the command to get your confirmation before the replacement takes place.

[LINE1],[LINE2] [?] S [STRING] Searches for string of characters but does not replace them.

[LINE] T [DRIVE][PATH] FILENAME Merges the contents of another file, read in from the disk, with the current file.

[N] W Writes portions of the file to disk. [N] specifies the number of lines to be written starting from the first line in memory.

EGA.SYS

☐ Operating System   ☐ Batch file   ■ Configuration

Description

This device driver is necessary if you are using an EGA monitor and you are running any program that involves task swapping, e.g. Windows or DOSSHELL. Its purpose is to refresh the display. It must be installed in the CONFIG.SYS.

Command Syntax

DEVICE=[DRIVE][PATH]EGA.SYS

Parameter Information

[DRIVE][PATH] Specifies the location of EGA.SYS.

Command Examples

1   **DEVICE=C:\DOS\EGA.SYS.**

Error Messages

There are no associated error messages.

EMM386.EXE

■ Operating System   ☐ Batch file   ■ Configuration

Description

EMM386 provides access to the high memory area on a computer that is based around the 80386 or 80486 chip. There is no point using it if you are only have an 80286 or lesser chip. The program can also be used for managing memory, either expanded or extended. There are a huge range of parameters that can be applied to this command, actually a program, but you will never use most of them.

Command Syntax

DEVICE=[DRIVE][PATH] EMM386.EXE [ON or OFF or AUTO] [AMOUNT] [W=ON or W=OFF] [M? or FRAME=ADDRESS or /PVALUE] [P?=ADDRESS] [X=MMMM-NNNN] [I=MMMM-NNNN] [B=ADDRESS] [L=MINXMS] [A=ALTREGS] [H=HANDLES] [D=NNN] [RAM] [NOEMS]

Parameter Information

[DRIVE][PATH] Specifies the location of the device driver.

[ON] Activates the device driver.

[OFF] Turns the device driver off.

[AUTO] Switches the device driver into automatic mode. This means that the program will only make expanded memory available if another program calls for it.

EMM386.EXE

[AMOUNT] Specifies the amount of memory that you want to use in kilobytes. The amount must be within the range 16 to 32768. in multiples of 16. The default is 256 which will be used if you do not express a value.

[W=ON] Turns on support for a Wietek co-processor.

[W=OFF] Turns off Wietek co-processor support. This is the default.

[M?] Specifies the address of the page frame. The value, which specifies a hexadecimal address, can be any of the following:

1 => C000	2 => C400	3 => C800
4 => CC00	5 => D000	6 => D400
7 => D800	8 => DC00	9 => E000
10 => 8000	11 => 8400	12 => 8800
13 => 8C00	14 => 9000	

Values 10 to 14, inclusive, can only be used on computers with 512 Kb of RAM.

[FRAME=ADDRESS] Specifies the page frame directly instead of using value. If you use this parameter you do not use the previous one.

[/PVALUE] Specifies the address of the page frame.

[P?=ADDRESS] Specifies the segment address of a specific page of memory. ? is the value of the page you want to use in the range 0 to 255. The ADDRESS, specified in hexadecimal, must be

EMM386.EXE

in the range 8000 to 9C00 and C000 through EC00 - in increments of 400.

[X=MMMM-NNNN] Stops EMM386 from using a range of memory locations, specified in hexadecimal, for an EMS page. Values range between A000 to FFFF. If you use this parameter it takes priority over the following one.

[I=MMMM-NNNN] As above but specifies a range to be used.

[B=ADDRESS] Specifies the lowest address available.

[L=MINXMS] Forces the device driver to use the amount of extended memory specified. The default value is 0.

[A=ALTREGS] Specifies fast alternate register sets for multitasking. Values range from 0 to 254. The default is 7. Each alternate register adds 200 bytes to the amount of RAM begin used by EMM386.

[H=HANDLES] The number of handles the program can use in the range 2 to 255. Default is 64.

[D=NNN] The amount of memory, in kilobytes, that will be reserved for direct memory access. Values can range from 16 to 256 with a default of 16.

[RAM] Provides access to both expanded memory and the upper memory area.

[NOEMS] Provides access to the upper memory area but disables access to expanded memory.

EMM386.EXE

Command Examples

Because **EMM386.EXE** has so many parameters you can get really complex with using it. However, the majority of people will not need to do this and can use the program at its simplest level - which works perfectly well with no problems.

1. **DEVICE=C:\DOS\EMM386.EXE NOEMS.** This simply loads the device driver and provides the access to the upper memory area so that other device drivers can be loaded there.

2. To check the status of the device driver just enter **EMM386** from the system prompt.

3. To emulate expanded memory you would include a line in the CONFIG.SYS saying **DEVICE=[DRIVE] [PATH] EMM386.EXE RAM**.

Error Messages

a. If the program cannot find 64 Kb of contiguous memory you will get the error message **Unable to set base address**.

b. If you use the parameters to the command incorrectly you may not get any error message - instead the computer system will lock up. In such a case you will need to use your Emergency Boot Disk to recover the situation.

223

EMM386.EXE

  c. If you try to use the program on any computer that has an 80286 or lesser chip you will get the error message **EMM386 not installed**.

Notes

  a. You must install HIMEM.SYS before using EMM386.EXE.

  b. EMM386.EXE cannot itself be installed into the High Memory Area. But it does allow other device drivers to be located there.

  c. To provide access to the upper memory area you must include either the RAM or NOEMS parameter.

  d. If you have installed EMM386.EXE you cannot run Windows in Standard Mode. However, running EMM386 reduces the amount of memory available in the machine and therefore you may not have enough left to run in 386-Enhanced mode. Try reducing the amount of memory allocated to other devices or omit some of them.

EXE2BIN.EXE

■ Operating System   ☐ Batch file   ☐ Configuration

Description

This program converts executable files, i.e. those with an EXE extension, into binary format. The program is not intended to be used by general users. To quote from Microsoft "EXE2BIN is included with MS-DOS as a courtesy to software developers." Isn't that nice of them?

Command Syntax

> **EXE2BIN** [DRIVE1][PATH] [FILE1] [DRIVE2][PATH] [FILE2]

Parameter Information

> [DRIVE1][PATH] Specifies the location of the file to be converted.
>
> [FILE1] The name of the file to be converted.
>
> [DRIVE2][PATH] Specifies the location for the converted file.
>
> [FILE2] The name of the converted file.

Command Examples

> 1   **EXE2BIN** [FILE1] [FILE2] This will convert file1 into binary format and then place it in the directory you are logged on to.

EXE2BIN.EXE

Error Messages

Not applicable.

Notes

a. Do not play with this program unless you know what you are doing.

EXIT

■ Operating System ☐ Batch file ☐ Configuration

Description

EXIT will terminate the current command interpreter and return you to the program that started it. For example, if you use the MS-DOS windows from within Windows it starts a second command processor. By entering **EXIT** you terminate this and return to the Windows environment.

Command Syntax

EXIT

Other Information

There are no parameters or error messages for this command.

227

EXPAND.EXE

■ Operating System ☐ Batch file ☐ Configuration

Description

The MS-DOS upgrade files are all compressed and as such cannot be used directly. You have to use this program to uncompress them and make them suitable for use.

Command Syntax

EXPAND [DRIVE][PATH] FILENAME [DRIVE][PATH]

Parameter Information

[DRIVE][PATH] Specifies the location of the file to be expanded.

[FILENAME] The name of the single file to be expanded. You cannot use wildcard characters and expand multiple files.

[DRIVE][PATH] The destination for the expanded file.

Command Examples

1   **EXPAND A:\FORMAT.CO_ C:\DOS** will take the FORMAT command off the upgrade disk and expand it into C:\DOS so that you can use it. Note that the extensions of the compressed files all end in an underline character.

EXPAND.EXE

Error Messages

There are no associated error messages other than the generic ones caused by mis-spelling or an invalid location.

Notes

a. **EXPAND** is really a fail-safe program that will allow you to unpack and load an accidentally lost program file. As such it is worth making a backup copy of it on your Emergency Boot Disk.

FASTOPEN.EXE

■ Operating System   ☐ Batch file   ■ Configuration

Description

FASTOPEN stores locations of files so that they can be accessed and loaded faster than would normally be the case. The program can either be run from the system prompt or you can have it installed in the CONFIG.SYS. You cannot use it on a network.

Command Syntax

FASTOPEN DRIVE [=N] [DRIVE][=N] ... [/x]

or to install the program in the CONFIG.SYS:

INSTALL=[DRIVE][PATH] **FASTOPEN.EXE** DRIVE [=N] [DRIVE] [=N] .. [/x]

or to install the program in the HMA via the AUTOEXEC.BAT:

LH [DRIVE][PATH] **FASTOPEN.EXE** DRIVE [=N] [DRIVE][=N] .. [/x]

Parameter Information

DRIVE You must specify at least one hard drive to load the program. You cannot use **FASTOPEN** with floppy disks.

[=N] Sets the number of files that the program can work with at the same time. The value can be between 10 and 999 with a default of 48 if you omit this parameter. Each file uses 48 bytes

FASTOPEN.EXE

of memory so that 10 files will use 480 bytes and 90 files will use 4,320 bytes.

[DRIVE] Specifies a second or subsequent drive for which **FASTOPEN** is to keep records. Each drive designator must include a colon after the drive letter. You can include as many drives as you need - up to 24 of them.

[/x] Creates the records in expanded memory rather than conventional memory.

LH The abbreviation for **LOADHIGH** which installs the program in the HMA.

Command Examples

1. To use the program with three drives and install it in the HMA you would have a line in the AUTOEXEC.BAT saying **LH C:\DOS\FASTOPEN C: D: E:**.

2. To use the program with a single drive and install it in the CONFIG.SYS you would have a line saying **INSTALL=C:\DOS\FASTOPEN.EXE C:**.

FASTOPEN.EXE

Error Messages

a. The only error message you are likely to see, other than the generic ones, is **FASTOPEN already installed**. You can only run the program once and thereafter cannot change any of the parameters except by rebooting the machine.

Notes

a. Whether or not it is worth using the program is somewhat debatable. The program really comes into its own if you are using databases because such programs do a lot of disk manipulation. If you just using a word processor or other non-disk intensive software then it may not be worth using. I suggest that you try using it for a while, then try doing without it and see if it makes a difference.

b. Do not try to run **FASTOPEN** from the **DOSSHELL** or from within Windows. If you do you so you will probably lock up the computer system.

c. Do not run a disk compression program while **FASTOPEN** is running.

FC.EXE

■ Operating System ❐ Batch file ❐ Configuration

Description

FC compares two files and reports on the differences between them.

Command Syntax

FC [/A] [/C] [/L] [/LBVALUE] [/N] [/T] [/W] [/NNN] [DRIVE1][PATH] FILE1 [DRIVE2][PATH] FILE2

or

FC /B [DRIVE1][PATH] FILE1 [DRIVE2][PATH] FILE2

Parameter Information

[/A] Causes the display of the differences between ASCII files to be shortened. Instead of displaying all the different lines, FC will only display the first and last lines.

[/C] Causes the program to ignore the cases of letters when doing the comparison.

[/L] Checks the files in ASCII mode line by line and then tries to synchronise the files after finding a difference.

[/LBVALUE] Specifies the number of lines for the internal line buffer used when comparing files. By default the VALUE is 100.

FC.EXE

[/N] Displays line numbers during the comparison.

[/T] Causes the program not to expand tabulations to spaces. By default tabs are treated as spaces.

[/W] Effectively ignores white space, i.e. tabs and spaces, by suppressing them. Consecutive spaces and/or tabs are treated as if they were a single space.

[/NNNN] Sets the number of consecutive lines that must match before the program defines the files as synchronised. By default this is 2.

[DRIVE1][PATH] Specifies the location of the first file.

[DRIVE2][PATH] Specifies the location of the second file.

[/B] Makes binary comparisons.

Command Examples

1. **FC C:\ALPHA\ALAN.DOC C:\BETA\ALAN.DOC** will compare two files, note that they each have the same filename and extension, to show the differences between them.

2. **FC C:\ALPHA*.DOC C:\BETA\ALAN.TXT** will compare all the files with an extension of .DOC, one after another, to the file called ALAN .TXT.

FC.EXE

Error Messages

a. The generic message **Cannot find file** will occur if you misspell or mis-specify the location of one of the files being compared.

b. If you enter **FC [FILE1] [FILE2]** as the files are compared you get a message something like this:

> ******* [FILE1]**
> **difference1**
> **difference2**
> ******* [FILE2]**
> **difference1**
> **difference2**
> *********

c. If the files being compared are too large, i.e. they do not fit within the line buffer and **FC** cannot find a match, you will get a message saying **Resynch failed. Files are too different**.

Notes

a. **FC** really comes into its own when you want to check different back-ups of files.

FCBS

☐ Operating System ☐ Batch file ■ Configuration

Description

Specifies the number of File Control Blocks that the operating system can have open at any one time.

Command Syntax

FCBS=N

Parameter Information

N The number of file control blocks that may be open. By default the value is 4 but it can range from 1 to 255.

Command Examples

1   **FCBS=10**. The line is included in the CONFIG.SYS.

Error Messages

Generic messages only.

FDISK.EXE

■ Operating System   ☐ Batch file   ☐ Configuration

Description

Before any hard disk can be used with MS-DOS it must be identified, via the machine BIOS, and configured to make it ready for use. **FDISK** is the program that does the latter.

Command Syntax

FDISK

Parameter Information

There are no parameters for this command.

Command Examples

1. Entering **FDISK** will bring up a full screen display, in monochrome, containing the following choices:

   FDISK options

   Current fixed disk drive: [1]
   1. Create DOS partition or Logical disk drive
   2. Set active partition
   3. Delete partition or Logical disk drive
   4. Display partition information
   Enter choice: [1]

FDISK.EXE

Note, that the first option is pre-selected so do not press **Enter**.

Try pressing **4-Enter** to see the current setup. Then **Esc** to return to the first screen. Pressing **Esc** again terminates **FDISK**.

Error Messages

There are no associated error messages.

Notes

a. You cannot use **FDISK** with any drive to which **ASSIGN, JOIN** or **SUBST** has been applied.

b. The maximum sized partition you can have with MS-DOS 5.0 is 2 Gigabytes.

c. Once you have run **FDISK**, the disk will still need to be formatted before it can be used.

d. WARNING: **FDISK** will destroy data very effectively. Be very careful about using it.

e. The options presented by **FDISK** are:

FDISK.EXE

1) Create DOS partition or Logical disk drive

A partition is, basically, an area of the hard disk that MS-DOS recognises as an individual disk drive. Once you select this option you will then have to input the size for the partition and MS-DOS will do the rest. If the disk is already partitioned then the operating system will tell you so and the entire process will terminate.

2) Change Active partition

Allows you to modify partitions already in existence. However do not do this if you have data on the disk or you will definitely lose it. One of the main reasons for changing the partitions is that you can have different operating systems on each one, e.g. MS-DOS on one and UNIX on another. But generally speaking once the partitions have been created in the first place you will not normally want to adjust them.

3) Delete DOS partition or Logical disk drive

Does exactly what it says and wipes out all the data in the partition in the process. You will then be unable to get at the data, although it still physically exists on the disk. You cannot recreate the partition once it has been deleted, all you can do is create another one of the same size.

4) Display Partition Data

This gives you a textual summary of the partitions on the disk so that you can see exactly what you have got.

FILES

☐ Operating System   ☐ Batch file   ■ Configuration

Description

This command which must be included in the CONFIG.SYS sets the number of files that the operating system may access at one time.

Command Syntax

FILES=n

Parameter Information

n Specifies the number of files. The value can range from 8 to 255. The default, set if you do not include the command in the CONFIG.SYS, will be 8.

Command Examples

1   **FILES=30** sets 30 files.

Error Messages

There are no associated error messages but if you set the number of files too low you may find that some programs will not work. Equally if you try to use more than 255 files a message appears telling you that the number is out of range and the default will be set.

FILES

Notes

a. For the majority of modern software you should set a value of at least 20. If you are using the Windows environment you should use 30.

b. The number of files depends on the type of program you are using. For example, using a database needs more than a word processor does.

c. Each file uses memory, about 60 bytes per additional file.

FIND.EXE

■ Operating System ☐ Batch file ☐ Configuration

Description

FIND is a utility program that allows you to search through files to find a specific string of text.

Command Syntax

FIND [/v] [/c] [/n] [/i] "STRING" [DRIVE][PATH] FILENAME

Parameter Information

[/v] Causes the command to display all the lines of the file that do not contain the string you are looking for.

[/c] Gives a count of the number of lines that contain the specified string.

[/N] Causes the displayed lines to be preceded by their line number, i.e. their position in the file.

[/I] Makes the search not case sensitive.

"STRING" The text for which you are searching. The string must be enclosed in quote marks.

[DRIVE][PATH] The location of the file being searched.

FIND.EXE

Command Examples

1   **FIND** /v /ı "ms-dos" **README.TXT** will search through the named file trying to find the phrase MS-DOS, in either lower or upper case. If you omit the /ı then the string being searched for must be identical to what you ask for.

Error Messages

a. There are no associated error messages.

Notes

a. You cannot use **FIND** to search for carriage returns - the program does not recognise them.

b. If you want to search for text that is enclosed in quotes you must double the quotes in the string, e.g. **"And he said, ""Hello, how are you"""**.

243

FOR

■ Operating System   ■ Batch file   ☐ Configuration

Description

An operator that runs a specified command a number of times on a set of files. The command is mainly used in batch files where it allows you to create interactive files.

Command Syntax

FOR %VARIABLE IN (SET) DO COMMAND [PARAMETERS]

Parameter Information

%VARIABLE Specifies a replaceable value. You must include the percentage sign. The **FOR** command replaces the variable with each text string until it has processed all the SET of files.

IN DO This is not a parameter - it must be included as it is part of the command.

(SET) Specifies the file(s) or the text string you want to process with the command. You must include the parentheses.

COMMAND [PARAMETERS] The command, and any particular parameters, you want to use.

FOR

Command Examples

1. **FOR %F IN (*.TXT) DO TYPE %F** will find each file in the current directory with an extension of .TXT and **TYPE** it to the screen.

Error Messages

a. Mis-using the command will cause the error message **Syntax error** to appear.

b. Mis-use of command parameters will cause the command's own associated error messages to appear.

Notes

a. **FOR** is really only used in batch files. It is unlikely to be used from the system prompt as such.

FORMAT.COM

■ Operating System ☐ Batch file ☐ Configuration

Description

Before any disk can be used for storing information it must be prepared so that MS-DOS can identify it. **FORMAT** is the command that does this. You cannot use this command on a networked system. Basically, the command lays down a series of circular tracks, one inside the other, and then divides these into arc shaped sectors. The sectors form the basis of all disk storage, which is normally allocated in Clusters, i.e. a multiple of the sectors. The command also creates the Root Directory and the File Allocation Tables.

Command Syntax

FORMAT DRIVE [/V:LABEL] [/Q] [/U] [F:SIZE] [/B] [/S]

or

FORMAT DRIVE [/V:LABEL] [/Q] [/U] [/T:TRACKS /N:SECTORS] [/B] [/S]

or

FORMAT DRIVE [/V:LABEL] [/Q] [/U] [/1] [/4] [/B] [/S]

or

FORMAT DRIVE [/Q] [/U] [/1] [/4] [/8] [/B] [/S]

FORMAT.COM

Parameter Information

DRIVE You must specify which drive is to be formatted.

[/V:LABEL] Allows you to give a name, i.e. a volume label, to the disk automatically. If you omit this parameter then you will be prompted to supply a volume label once the disk has been formatted. The LABEL can be up to 11 characters and may include blank spaces.

[/Q] The abbreviation for Quick. It does not actually format the disk but simply replaces the previous FAT and the root directory. In essence it renews the disks. You can only use this parameter on a disk that has previously been formatted.

[/U] Forces an unconditional format which will destroy all existing data and prevents you unformatting the disk later.

[/F:SIZE] Specifies the size of the disk to be formatted. If you omit this parameter then the command will try to format the disk to the maximum size possible in that disk drive. The available sizes are:

    160 Kb - as 160, 160k or 160kb
    180 Kb - as 180, 180k or 180kb
    320 Kb - as 320, 320k or 320 kb
    360 Kb - as 360, 360k or 360kb
    720 Kb - as 720, 720k or 720kb
    1.2 Mb - as 1200, 1200k, 1200kb, 1.2, 1.2m or 1.2 mb
    1.44 Mb - as 1440, 1440k, 1440kb, 1.44, 1.44m or 1.44mb
    2.88Mb - as 2880, 2880k, 2880kb, 2.88, 2.88m or 2.88mb

FORMAT.COM

[/T:TRACKS /N:SECTORS] Specifies the number of tracks and sectors to be placed on the disk. Ideally you should use /F:SIZE rather than this.

[/1] Formats a single side of the disk only.

[/4] Allows you to format a 360 Kb 5.25" disk in a 1.2 Mb disk drive.

[/8] Specifies that only 8 sectors are to be placed on a track.

[/B] Reserves space on the newly formatted disk for placing the system files, i.e. IO.SYS, MSDOS.SYS. You cannot use this parameter with the following one.

[/S] Copies the system files to disk. You cannot use this parameter with the previous one.

Command Examples

1. To format a disk in a drive to the maximum size possible just enter **FORMAT [DRIVE]**. Do not try formatting a low density disk to a high density capacity - you will only end up with damaged disks.

2. To format a 720 Kb disk in Drive-B, a 1.44 Mb drive, enter **FORMAT B: /F:720**.

FORMAT.COM

Error Messages

a. If you try to use the FORMAT command on a hard disk you will be shown a message saying **WARNING, ALL DATA ON NON-REMOVABLE DISK DRIVE ?: WILL BE LOST! Proceed with Format (Y/N)?** Press **Y** to continue or **N** to terminate the command.

b. You cannot use **FORMAT** on any drive that has had **ASSIGN**, **JOIN** or **SUBST** applied to it.

Notes

a. To speed up quick formatting use **FORMAT** /q/u.

b. **FORMAT** is another command that returns errorlevel codes. The codes are:

    0 The format was successful.

    3 Interrupted by Ctrl-C or Ctrl-Break.

    4 Fatal error.

    5 User pressed **N** in response to warning message for hard disk format.

Errorlevels 1 and 2 do not exist.

c. **FORMAT** now has a complementary program, **UNFORMAT**.

GOTO

☐ Operating System ■ Batch file ☐ Configuration

Description

Used within batch files to redirect an operation so that you can move from one part of a batch file to another. Extremely useful in interactive batch files – indeed it is vital.

Command Syntax

GOTO LABEL

Parameter Information

LABEL The name of the that part of the batch file you want to jump to. It may include spaces but not semi-colons or hyphens. You can use more than 8 characters for the name but only the first eight are taken into account. All LABEL names must begin with a colon.

Command Examples

1   **GOTO ALPHA** jumps to :ALPHA

Error Messages

Label not found is what appears if you try to use a missing name and the batch file terminates at that point.

GRAFTABL.COM

■ Operating System   ☐ Batch file   ☐ Configuration

Description

This program allows the operating system to display extended ASCII characters of a specified code page when in graphics mode.

Command Syntax

> **GRAFTABL [xxx]**
>
> or
>
> **GRAFTABL /STATUS**

Parameter Information

[xxx] Specifies the code table you wish to use. The valid codes are as follows:

- 437 United States
- 850 Multilingual (Latin 1)
- 852 Slavic (Latin II)
- 860 Portuguese
- 863 Canadian-French
- 865 Nordic

/STATUS Identifies the page and tells you what it is.

GRAFTABL.COM

Command Examples

1. **GRAFTABL**/STATUS will display the current selected code page.

2. **GRAFTABL 863** will set the Canadian-French code pages.

3. **GRAFTABL** entered by itself will load the relevant code page based on your current **COUNTRY** code settings.

Error Messages

a. **Active code page: None** is the message normally displayed when you enter **GRAFTABL**/STATUS without having previously loaded any code page.

b. **Previous code page: None Active code page: 437** is the message that appears when you enter the command by itself on a machine based in and for the UK.

Notes

a. **GRAFTABL** returns errorlevel codes as follows:

   0 Character set successfully loaded and no previous page was loaded prior.

GRAFTABL.COM

   1 Character set already loaded and replaced by new table.

   2 A file occur was encountered.

   3 Incorrect parameter - no action taken.

   4 Incorrect MS-DOS version - you must use Version 5.0.

b. **GRAFTABL** uses memory and will decrease the amount of available RAM by approximately 1 Kb.

GRAPHICS.COM

■ Operating System   ☐ Batch file   ☐ Configuration

Description

GRAPHICS will load a program into memory that will allow the operating system to print the displayed screen characters when you are using a colour monitor. Standards supported are CGA, EGA and VGA.

Command Syntax

GRAPHICS [TYPE] [DRIVE][PATH] [FILENAME] [/R] [/B] [/LCD] [/PRINTBOX:STD or /PRINTBOX:LCD]

Parameter Information

[TYPE] Specifies the type of printer to be used and it can be any of the following:

> COLOR1 IBM Personal Computer Color Printer with black ribbon only.
> COLOR4 IBM Personal Computer Color Printer with RGB and black ribbon.
> COLOR8 IBM Personal Computer Color Printer with CMYK ribbon.
> HPDEFAULT Any Hewlett-Packard PCL printer.
> DESKJET A HP DeskJet printer.
> GRAPHICS An IBM Personal graphics printer, Proprinter or Quietwriter.

GRAPHICS.COM

    GRAPHICSWIDE An IBM Personal Graphics printer with a wide carriage, i.e. 11".
    LASERJET An HP LaserJet.
    LASERJETII An HP LaserJet II.
    PAINTJET An HP PaintJet printer.
    QUIETJET An HP QuietJet printer.
    QUIETJETPLUS An HP QuietJet Plus.
    RUGGEDWRITER An HP RuggedWriter printer.
    RUGGEDWRITERWIDE An HP RuggedWriterwide printer.
    THERMAL AN IBM PC-convertible Thermal printer.
    THINKJET An HP ThinkJet printer.

[DRIVE][PATH] Specifies the location of the printer profile file to be used.

[FILENAME] Specifies the name of the printer profile to be used. If this is omitted then the operating system will use the file called **PRINTER.PRO** which must be in the current directory.

[/R] Causes the image to be printed exactly as it appears on screen, i.e. white on black. By default the command works the other way round, i.e. black on white.

[/B] Prints the background in colour - on the **COLOR4** and **COLOR8** options only.

[/LCD] Prints the image using LCD aspect ratio rather than the CGA ration.

[/PRINTBOX:STD] or **[/PRINTBOX:LCD]** Selects the print box size.

GRAPHICS.COM

Command Examples

1. To prepare to print graphics just enter **GRAPHICS**. Then you can press **Shift-PrintScreen** to actually do so.

Error Messages

a. The main errors are likely to be those caused by mis-spelling any of the parameters.

b. If you already have a printer profile loaded and you change to another one, then the new one must be smaller than the existing one. If not you get an error message saying **Unable to reload with profile supplied**.

Notes

a. Using **GRAPHICS** will reduce the amount of RAM available for other purposes because it stays loaded until you reboot.

HELP.EXE

■ Operating System   ☐ Batch file   ☐ Configuration

Description

A very simple textual account of what some of the commands do. It does not give information about a command per se, unless you enter the command with which you want assistance.

Command Syntax

HELP

or

HELP [COMMAND]

Parameter Information

[COMMAND] Can be any of the MS-DOS commands but not device drivers.

Command Examples

1   To get help with **FORMAT** you enter **HELP FORMAT** or use the shortcut **FORMAT/?**. The latter is a little bit faster at displaying the information.

HIMEM.SYS

☐ Operating System ☐ Batch file ■ Configuration

Description

The **HIMEM.SYS** device driver is what manages the extended memory of the machine. You must load this first if you want to use EMM386. The device driver also allows use of the HMA.

Command Syntax

> **DEVICE**=[DRIVE][PATH] **HIMEM.SYS** [/HMAMIN=?] [/NUMHANDLES=?] [/INT15=XXX] [/MACHINE:?] [/A20CONTROL:ON or OFF] [/SHADOWRAM:ON or OFF] [/CPULOCK:ON or OFF]

Parameter Information

[DRIVE][PATH] Specifies the location of HIMEM.SYS.

[/HMAMIN=?] The amount of memory, in kilobytes, that any program must be using before HIMEM.SYS will allow it into the HMA. Values range from 0 to 63 with a default of 0.

[/NUMHANDLES=?] The maximum number of extended memory block handles that can be used at the same time. Acceptable values range from 1 to 128 and the default is 32. Each additional handle uses an extra 6 bytes of memory.

[/INT15=XXX] Allocates the amount of extended memory, again in kilobytes, for the Interrupt 15h interface. The values can range from 64 to 65535 with a default of 0.

HIMEM.SYS

[/MACHINE:?] Specifies the A20 handler to be used, i.e. that part of the of the computer system that gives access to the HMA. Different machines use different values. You are only likely to need to set this parameter if you use one of the following machines, the **?** can be expressed as a code or a number:

AT	1	IBM PC/AT - the default
PS2	2	IBM PS/2
PT1CASCADE	3	Phoenix Cascade BIOS
HPVECTRA	4	HP Vectra A and A+
ATT6300PLUS	5	AT&T 6300 Plus
ACER1100	6	Acer 1100
TOSHIBA	7	Toshiba 1600 and 1200XE
WYSE	8	Wyse 12.5 MHz 286
TULIP	9	Tulip SX
ZENITH	10	Zenith ZBIOS
AT1	11	IBM PC/AT
AT2	12	IBM PC/AT alternate delay
CSS	12	CSS Labs
AT3	13	IBM PC/AT alternate delay
PHILIPS	13	Philips
FASTHP	14	HP Vectra

[/A20CONTROL:ON or OFF] Forces the device driver to take the A20 control line even if it was in use prior to HIMEM.SYS being loaded. The default is On.

[/SHADOWRAM:ON or OFF] Specifies whether or not HIMEM is to turn the shadow RAM on or off. If your machine has less then 2 Mb of RAM then the default is Off.

259

HIMEM.SYS

[/CPULOCK ON or OFF] Specifies whether or not HIMEM is allowed to affect the clock speed of the machine. Using this parameter will slow down the operation of HIMEM.SYS.

Command Examples

1   The simplest way to HIMEM is to place a line in your CONFIG.SYS saying **DEVICE=C:\DOS\HIMEM.SYS** and allow it to sort out how it will work.

Error Messages

a. You may encounter an error message saying **Unable to use A20 handler**. If so you should try setting the [/MACHINE=?] parameter to try and correct the problem.

Notes

a. [/SHADOWRAM:ON or OFF] will only work on some computers.

IF

☐ Operating System ■ Batch file ☐ Configuration

Description

IF is an operand that allows you to perform conditional processes within batch programs.

Command Syntax

IF [NOT] [ERRORLEVEL NUMBER] [STRING1==STRING2] [EXIST FILENAME] COMMAND

Parameter Information

[NOT] Reverses the meaning of the statement so that the statement must be false for the operation to continue.

[ERRORLEVEL NUMBER] Specifies an errorlevel number to be operated upon.

[STRING1==STRING2] The two strings, which must be separated by double equals signs, must be identical for the statement to be true. If you put [NOT] in from of the statement then the strings must not be identical.

[EXIST FILENAME] Means does the filename exist. If it does then the statement is true, if it doesn't then it is false.

COMMAND What you want to happen as a result of the conditional statement.

IF

Command Examples

1. **IF ERRORLEVEL=3 GOTO ALPHA** checks that the reported errorlevel, from running another program, is equal to or greater than 3 and if so causes the batch file to jump to the label ALPHA.

Error Messages

a. Any error messages will result from the conditional statements or from mis-spelling or grammar.

Notes

a. It is this statement more than any other that allows you to create interactive batch files.

b. Errorlevels have to be listed backwards, i.e. in reverse order, because the statement errorlevel=3 means "if the errorlevel is 3 or more". Thus if you had two lines, the first asking for errorlevel1 and the second for errorlevel 2 the second line would never be reached because it the first line is asking for an errorlevel of 1 or more. However, if you reverse the lines so that the first asks for errorlevel2 and the second asks for errorlevel 1 then the batch file will work.

INSTALL

☐ Operating System   ☐ Batch file   ■ Configuration

Description

Allows you to load memory software, either from MS-DOS or from third parties, into the memory as part of the boot up operation.

Command Syntax

>   INSTALL=[DRIVE][PATH] FILENAME [PARAMETERS]

Parameter Information

>   [DRIVE][PATH] Specifies the location of the filename that is to be loaded into memory.
>
>   FILENAME The program to be loaded.
>
>   [PARAMETERS] Any parameters that apply to filename.

Command Examples

>   1   **INSTALL=C:\DOS\FASTOPEN.EXE C:=50** installs the FASTOPEN program.

INSTALL

Error Messages

a. The only error message you are likely to encounter, other than the generic ones, is **Unable to load [filename]** or **File not found** because you have specified an incorrect location.

b. Secondary error messages will result from misuse of the filename parameters.

Notes

a. **INSTALL** is used in the CONFIG.SYS and as such you cannot use it to load programs into the HMA. Alternatively, with some programs, you may use LOADHIGH in the AUTOEXEC.BAT. The latter operation uses slightly more memory but allows access to the HMA which offsets this.

IO.SYS

■ Operating System ◻ Batch file ◻ Configuration

Description

IO.SYS is the first of the three main operating system files - without this the operating system won't work.

Command Syntax

There is no command syntax because the program is loaded automatically when the machine boots up.

Parameter Information

There are no parameters.

Error Messages

a. IO.SYS does not produce error messages as such. If anything happens to it then the computer will not boot up and you may not even get an error message - just a blank, dead screen.

JOIN.EXE

■ Operating System ☐ Batch file ☐ Configuration

Description

JOIN allows you to attach a disk drive to a directory on another disk drive. When you use this command the operating system treats the files on the disk drive as if they were within the directory of the second drive.

Command Syntax

    JOIN [DRIVE1:[DRIVE2]PATH**]**

    or

    JOIN/D

Parameter Information

[DRIVE1] This is the disk drive that is being joined to another. It can be any floppy disk drive or a logical partition.

[DRIVE2] This is the disk drive, again it can be any floppy or logical drive, that the first drive is being joined to.

[PATH] The directory that you want DRIVE1 to attach to. There are two rules about this directory; (1) It must be empty before you join anything to it, and (2) It must not be the root directory of DRIVE2.

JOIN.EXE

[/D] Cancels any joins in operation.

Command Examples

1. **JOIN B: C:\ALPHA** will join the floppy drive, B, to the sub-directory of Drive-C called ALPHA.

Error Messages

a. If the drive you have specified as DRIVE1 should become invalid for any reason, e.g. because it does not have a disk in it, then you will get an error message saying **Invalid drive specification**.

b. If the sub-directory being joined to is not empty then you get an error message saying **Directory not empty** and the command is terminated.

Notes

a. You cannot use **ASSIGN, BACKUP, CHKDSK, DISKCOMP, DISKCOPY, FDISK, FORMAT, LABEL, MIRROR, RECOVER, RESTORE** or **SYS** with any drive that has **JOIN** applied to it.

b. If you enter **JOIN** by itself you will be given a list of currently active joins.

267

KEYB.COM

□ Operating System   □ Batch file   ■ Configuration

Description

KEYB is responsible for configuring your keyboard to specific national characteristics. It can be installed in either the CONFIG.SYS or the AUTOEXEC.BAT. You don't have to use it but if you don't your keyboard will operate as an American one, e.g. you get a hash sign (#) instead of a pound sign (£) when you press **Shift-3**.

Command Syntax

[LH] [DRIVE][PATH] **KEYB** cc, [CODEPAGE], [DRIVE][PATH] **KEYBOARD.SYS** [/E] [/ID:NNN] in the AUTOEXEC.BAT,

or

INSTALL=[DRIVE][PATH] **KEYB** cc, [CODEPAGE], [DRIVE][PATH] **KEYBOARD.SYS** [/E] [/ID:NNN] in the CONFIG.SYS.

Parameter Information

[LH] The abbreviation for **LOADHIGH** which allows you to load the keyboard driver into the HMA.

[DRIVE][PATH] The first occurrence specifies the location of **KEYB.COM**. The second use specifies the location of **KEYBOARD.SYS**.

KEYB.COM

cc The keyboard country code that you want to use - and you must use one of them. It can be any of the following, with their associated code pages:

BE	Belgium	850,437
BR	Brazil	850,437
CF	Canadian-French	850,863
CZ	Czechoslovakia (Czech)	852,850
DK	Denmark	850,865
FR	France	850,437
GR	Germany	850,437
HU	Hungary	852,850
IT	Italy	850,437
LA	Latin-America	850,437
NL	Netherlands	850,437
NO	Norway	850,865
PL	Poland	852,850
PR	Portugal	850,860
SF	Switzerland (French)	850,437
SG	Switzerland (German)	850,437
SL	Czechoslovakia (Slavic)	852,850
SP	Spain	850,437
SU	Finland	850,437
SV	Sweden	850,437
UK	Britain	850,437
US	United States America	850,437
YU	Yugoslavia	852,850

[CODEPAGE] Specifies which code page you want to use.

KEYB.COM

[/E] This parameter means that you have an enhanced keyboard installed, i.e. one with 101 or 102 keys. You only need to use this if you are using a machine based on any 8088 or 8086 with such a keyboard.

[/ID:NNN] Specifies the keyboard layout in use. You only need this for those countries that have more then one layout for the same language, i.e. France - 120,189, Italy - 141,142 and the UK - 166,168.

Command Examples

1   LH **C:\DOS\KEYB.UK,,C:\DOS\KEYBOARD.SYS** sets the UK keyboard via the AUTOEXEC.BAT. Notice that the line includes two commas, which would normally separate the country code page from the country code itself: these must be included.

2   **INSTALL=C:\DOS\KEYB UK,,C:\DOS\KEYBOARD .SYS** does the same thing but installs the drivers via the CONFIG.SYS.

Error Messages

a. The only error message, other than the generic ones, is **File not found** caused by either KEYB.COM or KEYBOARD.SYS not being where you said they were.

KEYB.COM

Notes

a. If you use code pages you must have this installed on your system.

b. **KEYB** produces errorlevel codes:

   0 Keyboard drivers loaded successfully.

   1 Invalid country code, code page or syntax error.

   2 Keyboard definition file missing or damaged.

   4 Error while communicating with keyboard.

   5 Code page not prepared.

LABEL.EXE

■ Operating System   ☐ Batch file   ☐ Configuration

Description

LABEL allows you to apply a name, also called a volume label, to any disk.

Command Syntax

> **LABEL** [DRIVE] [NAME]

Parameter Information

> [DRIVE] Can be any disk drive that contains a disk or any physical or logical partition.
>
> [NAME] The name to be applied to the disk.

Command Examples

1. **LABEL C:DRIVE-C** will change the name of the primary partition to DRIVE-C.

2. Entering **LABEL C:** by itself will bring up the following:

   > Volume in drive C is existing name
   > Volume Serial Number is 1719-9BE3
   > Volume label (11 characters, ENTER for none)?

LABEL.EXE

The Serial Number will be different to that above because each one is distinct and impossible to duplicate. You can now enter any eleven characters you want, including a blank space. Pressing **Enter** will thereafter will apply the name.

To leave the name unchanged just press **Enter**. You will then asked **Delete current volume label (Y/N)?** Pressing **Y** deletes the old label and leaves a blank one there. Pressing **N** leaves the old label unchanged.

Error Messages

a. If you try to use an invalid character then you get an error message saying **Invalid characters in volume label** and then you are given the third line as above again.

Notes

a. Invalid characters for use in volume labels are: " ^ & * ( ) + = [ ] : ; | \ , . < > ? /

LASTDRIVE

☐ Operating System ☐ Batch file ■ Configuration

Description

By default MS-DOS can see and communicate with up to five drives, whether physical drives or logical partitions. On most systems this is more than adequate, especially as MS-DOS 5.0 will allow you to have a single partition of up to 2 Gigabytes! However, you may prefer to sub-divide your hard disk into smaller chunks and so end up with more than five drives. If you do so you have to include a line in the CONFIG.SYS telling the operating system how many drives you now have on the system. The maximum number of drives you can have is 26, one for each letter of the alphabet.

Command Syntax

   LASTDRIVE=?

Parameter Information

   ? Can be any letter of the alphabet. By default it will be E, giving you five drives and so if you have five drives or less you can ignore this command.

Command Examples

   1   **LASTDRIVE=I** allows you to have 9 distinct drives.

LASTDRIVE

Error Messages

There are no associated error messages. If you use two letters, e.g. GO then the command only recognises the first one.

Notes

a. Do not set more drives than you need because each additional letter uses up memory, about 100 bytes for each extra letter.

LOADFIX.COM

■ Operating System ☐ Batch file ☐ Configuration

Description

This program allows you to load another program above the first 64 Kb of RAM and then run the program from there. It will probably never have to be used.

Command Syntax

LOADFIX [DRIVE][PATH] FILENAME

Parameter Information

[DRIVE][PATH] Specifies the location of the program to be loaded.

FILENAME The program to be loaded.

Command Examples

1   **LOADFIX ALPHA.EXE** will load the named program above the first 64 Kb of memory.

Error Messages

a. There are no associated error messages but you would use this program if you got an error message from another program saying **Packed file corrupt** when you tried to run it.

LOADHIGH

☐ Operating System   ☐ Batch file   ■ Configuration

Description

Used in the AUTOEXEC.BAT, this command allows you to load device drivers or other programs into the High Memory Area. It can be abbreviated to just LH.

Command Syntax

LOADHIGH [DRIVE][PATH] [PROGRAM] [PARAMETERS]

Parameter Information

[DRIVE][PATH] Specifies the location of the program or device driver to be loaded.

[PROGRAM] The program or device driver to be loaded.

[PARAMETERS] The parameters for the program.

Command Examples

1 **LH C:\DOS\KEYB UK,,C:\DOS\KEYBOARD.SYS**
   loads the keyboard definition programs into the high memory area.

LOADHIGH

Error Messages

a. Any error message is likely to arise as a result of misuse of the program and/or its parameters.

Notes

a. Before you can use **LOADHIGH** you must include a line saying **DOS=[HIGH],UMB** in your CONFIG.SYS or you cannot load programs into the HMA. Equally you must also have a line in the CONFIG.SYS giving you access to the HMA. This is provided by the EMM386.EXE program.

b. If you have used up all the space in the HMA then any program you try to load thereafter will be loaded into the conventional memory area.

MEM.EXE

■ Operating System ☐ Batch file ☐ Configuration

Description

MEM allows you to examine the memory and how it is allocated to which programs. It also gives a report on the amount of unused memory remaining.

Command Syntax

MEM [/PROGRAM] [/DEBUG] [/CLASSIFY]

Parameter Information

[/PROGRAM] Using this parameter the command will display the address, name, size and type of programs loaded into the memory. It can be shorted to /P.

[/DEBUG] Gives mores detailed information than the previous parameter. It can be shorted to /D.

[/CLASSIFY] Gives the name and sizes of program loaded into the memory, sub-divided into the conventional and high memory areas. It can be shorted to /C.

Command Examples

1   **MEM**/c will give information about the two memory types. Unfortunately you will lose the first part of the

MEM.EXE

display. Therefore you should add |**MORE** to the end of the command which causes the display to be presented in 23 line chunks. When you do so you will get something like this:

Conventional Memory:

Name	Size in Decimal		Size in Hex
MSDOS	14160	(13.8K)	3750
HIMEM	1184	(1.2K)	4A0
EMM386	8400	(8.2K)	20D0
COMMAND	2624	(2.6K)	A40
DOSKEY	4128	(4.0K)	1020
FREE	64	(0.1K)	40
FREE	144	(0.1K)	90
FREE	624416	(609.8K)	98720

Total FREE: 624624   (610.0K)

Upper Memory:

Name	Size in Decimal		Size in Hex
SYSTEM	180224	(176.0K)	2C000
SMARTDRV	17904	(17.5K)	45F0
KEYB	6208	(6.1K)	1840
FREE	128	(0.1K)	80
FREE	57584	(56.2K)	E0F0

Total FREE: 57712   (56.4K)

Total bytes available to programs: 682335 (666.3K)
Largest executable program size: 624416 (609.8K)
Largest available upper memory block: 57584 (56.2K)

MEM.EXE

   1441792 bytes total contiguous extended memory
         0 bytes available contiguous extended memory
    814080 bytes available XMS memory
            MS-DOS resident in high memory area

2.   Entering **MEM** by itself will give you a report that tells you how much conventional memory is available and the largest executable programs size plus the last four lines above.

Error Messages

a.   The only error messages will be due to mis-spelling.

Notes

a.   **Total contiguous extended memory** is the total amount of RAM over and above the 1 Mb base amount.

b.   **Available contiguous memory** is extended memory available for the Interrupt 15h interface.

c.   **Available XMS memory** is the amount of RAM being managed by **HIMEM.SYS**.

MIRROR.COM

■ Operating System ☐ Batch file ☐ Configuration

Description

MIRROR is one of the utilities licensed from Central Point Software, it is one part of PC Tools. Its purpose is to record information about files on the disk(s) which can then be used to recover from an accidental format, or to recover lost files.

Command Syntax

MIRROR [drive] [/1] [/tdrive [-entries]]

or

MIRROR [/u]

or

MIRROR [/partn]

Parameter Information

[drive] The drive, which must contain a disk, that you want **MIRROR** to save information about. The information, containing details of the FAT and root directory, is written to the disk in a hidden file called MIRORSAV.FIL and a visible file called MIRROR.FIL.

MIRROR.COM

[/1] Causes the command to keep only one record of the information. Normally when you run **MIRROR** a second time, the first set of data is renamed to MIRROR.BAK. If you use this parameter that does not occur.

[/TDRIVE [-ENTRIES]] Loads a memory resident program that is used by the **UNDELETE** program to recover files. You must include the **DRIVE** part, which specifies the drive for which information is to be retained, but **[-ENTRIES]** is optional. This part of the command must be a value in the range 1 to 999 and it specifies the maximum number of entries to be allowed for.

[/U] Unloads the memory resident part of the program. However, you cannot do this if you have loaded any other memory resident program after MIRROR.

[/PARTN] Save disk partition information to a floppy disk, by default this will be Drive-A. You cannot, or should not, save partition information to a hard disk for obvious reasons.

Command Examples

1. Entering **MIRROR** from the system prompt saves information about the current drive. It should be run often - the more often you run it the better your chances of recovering data.

2. **LH MIRROR/T C:** loads the memory resident part of the program into the high memory area from where it automatically keeps a check on erased data files.

MIRROR.COM

You can exclude the additional parameter because MIRROR can use its owns defaults depending on the disks size as follows:

Disk Size	Entries	File Size
360 Kb	25	5 Kb
720 Kb	50	9 Kb
1.2 Mb	75	14 Kb
1.44 Mb	75	14 Kb
20 Mb	101	18 Kb
32 Mb	202	36 Kb
32 Mb plus	303	55 Kb

Error Messages

a. When you run the MIRROR program you get a message saying **Drive ? being processed** as the data is checked and recorded and then you are told **The MIRROR process was successful**.

b. If for any reason the program is unable to write the data file to disk you will get a message saying **The MIRROR process was unsuccessful**.

Notes

a. You cannot use **[/TDRIVE]** on any drive that has had **JOIN** or **SUBST** applied to it. If you want to use **ASSIGN** on a drive you must do so before you use **MIRROR**.

MKDIR

■ Operating System ☐ Batch file ☐ Configuration

Description

MKDIR is the command that allows you to create directories. The command can be abbreviated to just **MD**.

Command Syntax

MKDIR [DRIVE] [PATH] [NAME]

Parameter Information

[DRIVE] Allows you to create a directory on any drive other than the one you are currently logged on to.

[PATH] Allows you to add a directory to the specified path.

[NAME] Can be any string of up to eleven characters, eight for the main name and three for the extension, excepting the reserved words and characters.

Command Examples

1   **MD C:\ALPHA** will create a directory called ALPHA subtended off the root directory of Drive-C.

MKDIR

2   **MD D:\MERCURY\REPORT.001** creates a directory called REPORT.001 subtended off a directory called Mercury on Drive-D. It is unusual to give directories extensions but there is no reason why you should not.

Error Messages

a. **Directory already exists** is the message that appears if you try to create a directory of the same name on the same drive or directory.

b. **Unable to create directory** will appear due to syntax errors.

Notes

a. You cannot have two directories of the same name subtended off the same directory.

MODE.COM

■ Operating System　　☐ Batch file　　☐ Configuration

Description

MODE can be used to configure system devices, the ports, code pages, display adapters and the keyboard rate. For each of these there are different parameters. Generally speaking, you will probably never have to use the command because the defaults will work exceptionally well. The only time you might need to use the command is if you have a machine that has a strange configuration or you want to utilise a completely different configuration.

Command Syntax

a) **MODE** LPT? [:] [COLS=C] [LINES=L] [RETRY=R] to configure printer.

b) **MODE** COM? [:] [BAUD=B] [PARITY=P] [DATA=D] [STOP=S] [RETRY=R] to configure the serial ports.

c) **MODE** [DEVICE] [/STATUS] to display the status of a device.

d) **MODE** LPT? [:]=COM?[:] to redirect printing.

e) **MODE** DEVICE CODEPAGE PREPARE= ((YYY [...]) [DRIVE][PATH] FILENAME) to prepare device code pages.

f) **MODE** DEVICE CODEPAGE SELECT=YYY to select a code page for a device.

g) **MODE** DEVICE CODEPAGE REFRESH To refresh the code page on a device.

287

MODE.COM

h) **MODE** DEVICE CODEPAGE [/STATUS] to check the status of a device.

i) **MODE** [DISPLAY] [,SHIFT[,T]] to set the display mode.

j) MODE CON[:] [RATE=R DELAY=D] to set the keyboard repeat rate.

Parameter Information

LPT? Specifies the parallel port to which the printing device it connected. **?** can be 1, 2 or 3.

[COLS=C] Specifies the number of columns per line, 80 or 132. The default is the former.

[LINES=L] The number of lines per inch, 6 or 8. The default is 6.

COM? Specifies the COM port to be configured. **?** can be 1 to 4.

[BAUD=B] Sets the transmission rate in bits per second. B is a two-digit number as follows:

11	110 baud	12	1200 baud
15	150 baud	19	19200 baud
24	2400 baud	30	300 baud
48	4800 baud	60	600 baud
96	9600 baud		

[PARITY=P] Specifies the parity check. P can be N - none, E - even, O - odd, M - mark or S - space. Note, some machines cannot use M or S.

MODE.COM

[DATA=D] The number of data bits per character. D can be any digit in the range 5 to 8 with a default of 7. Note, some machines do not support 5 and 6.

[STOP=S] The number of stop bits. s can be 1, 1.5 or 2. If the baud rate is set to 100 then the default stop bit setting is 2, otherwise it is 1.

[RETRY=R] The action that will be taken if a time-out error occurs. R can be any of the following:

B	Return "busy" from a busy port.
E	Return an error from a busy port.
N	Take no action.
P	Continuing retrying.
R	Return "ready" from a busy port.

[DEVICE] Specifies the device you want to know the status of.

[/STATUS] Requests the status of any redirected printers. It can be shortened to /STA.

LPT? Specifies the parallel port to be redirected. ? can be any of the following 1, 2 or 3.

COM? The communications port to which the printing is to be redirected. Values can be 1, 2, 3 or 4.

MODE.COM

DEVICE The device for which you want to prepare or select a code page.

CODEPAGE PREPARE Prepares the code page for use. The code page, which can be shortened to **CP**, must be prepared before it can be used.

YYY The number of the code page you want to prepare or select. It must be one of the following:

437	United States	850	Multilingual (Latin I)
852	Slavic (Latin II)	860	Portuguese
863	Canadian-French	865	Nordic

[DRIVE][PATH] FILENAME The location and name of the code page information file. MS-DOS 5.0 comes complete with five .CPI files as follows:

4201.CPI	IBM Proprinter II and III Model 4201.
	IBM Proprinter II and III Model 4202.
4208.CPI	IBM Proprinter X24E Model 4207.
	IBM Proprinter XL24E Model 4208.
5202.CPI	IBM Quietwriter III.
EGA.CPI	EGA monitor or IBM PS/2.
LCD.CPI	IBM liquid crystal display.

CODEPAGE SELECT Selects the code page to be used. It must have been prepared before use.

CODEPAGE REFRESH Restores the code page if it has been lost for any reason.

MODE.COM

[/STATUS] Displays the status of the code page. It can be shortened to /STA.

[DISPLAY] Sets the classification for the display. It can be any of the following values:

    40   Sets 40 characters per line and large characters.
    80   Sets the standard 80 characters per line.
    BW40 Disables the colour and gives 40 cpl.
    BW80 Display the colour and gives 80 cpl.
    CO40 Enables the colour and gives 40 cpl.
    CO80 Enables the colour and gives 80 cpl.
    MONO Gives monochrome and 80 cpl.

[,SHIFT] Will shift the display to the left (L) or the right (R).

[,T] Allows the screen to be aligned using a test pattern.

CON Specifies the monitor.

[RATE=R] The rate at which the character reappears on the screen when you press a key. R can be any value in the range 1 to 32 with a default of 20.

[DELAY=D] The delay time before a character is repeated. The range for D can be 1, 2, 3 or 4 and it applies to 0.25 second increments. It you set a rate you must set a delay as well.

MODE.COM

Command Examples

1. To set a printer on LPT2 to print 80 columns and 8 lines per inch you enter **MODE LPT2:80,8**.

2. To set COM Port 2 to use a baud rate of 9600 you could enter **MODE COM2 BAUD=96**.

3. To see the status of all devices connected to the system enter **MODE |MORE**. (The **|MORE** is needed because the display will scroll off the screen.)

4. To redirect printing from LPT1 to COM2 enter **MODE LPT1=COM2**.

5. **MODE 40** changes the monitor to give 40 characters per line and large characters.

Error Messages

a. Error messages depend on misuse of the command, generally syntax errors.

MODE.COM

Notes

a. The main occasions you are likely to need to use mode is when a program crashes out and leaves you with a changed display. Entering **MODE 80** will normally fix this. However, you should reboot to be on the safe side.

MORE.COM

■ Operating System   ☐ Batch file   ☐ Configuration

Description

MORE allows you to stop the screen display so that after giving you 23 lines of textual information it pauses and displays -- **more** -- until you press any key. You will then be given the next 23 lines and so on. The data to be viewed must be redirected somehow to use this command.

Command Syntax

>   **MORE** < [DRIVE][PATH] FILENAME
>
> or
>
>   COMMAND |**MORE**

Parameter Information

> **<** Works with viewing files only. Has the same effect as **TYPE |MORE** [FILENAME].
>
> [DRIVE][PATH] Specifies the location of the file to be viewed.
>
> FILENAME The file to be viewed.
>
> COMMAND You can use **|MORE** with **DIR**, **SORT** or **TYPE**. You must include the | character, which is called a pipe.

MORE.COM

Command Examples

1. **MORE < README.TXT** will display the file called README.TXT on the screen in chunks of 23 lines. Press any key to view the next 23 lines.

2. **TYPE README.TXT |MORE** does exactly the same thing.

3. **DIR |MORE** has the same effect as **DIR/P**.

Error Messages

a. The only errors are likely to be the generic ones.

Notes

a. **MORE** is such a useful command that I recommend that you include it on your Emergency Boot Disk.

MSHERC.COM

■ Operating System   ☐ Batch file   ☐ Configuration

Description

This program simply allows you to use a Hercules graphics card with the QBasic programs.

Command Syntax

> **MSHERC** [HALF]

Parameter Information

> [HALF] Allows you to run the command even when a colour adaptor is installed on the system.

Command Examples

> 1   **MSHERC** runs the program.

Error Messages

> a. Generic messages only.

Notes

> a. If you don't have a Hercules monitor delete this program.

NLSFUNC.EXE

■ Operating System   ☐ Batch file   ☐ Configuration

Description

NLSFUNC loads country specific information. You will probably never have to use it. The program can be run from the system prompt or it can be installed in the CONFIG.SYS.

Command Syntax

> **NLSFUNC** [DRIVE][PATH] FILENAME
>
> or
>
> **INSTALL=**[DRIVE][PATH] **NLSFUNC.EXE** [COUNTRY]

Parameter Information

> [DRIVE][PATH] Specifies the location of the file.
>
> [COUNTRY] The file containing the country specific information.

Command Examples

1. To use the default country information, i.e that set by the COUNTRY.SYS file, just enter **NLSFUNC**.

2. If you have a data file that contains country information you want to use then enter **NLSFUNC filename**.

PATH

■ Operating System ☐ Batch file ☐ Configuration

Description

The **PATH** defines a list of sub-directories in which the operating system can, and will, search for the program files you request - regardless of where you issue a command from. Whenever you type something at the system prompt, MS-DOS assumes it is a command. It always searches through the current directory, i.e. the one you are logged on to, looking for a program name that matches what you have entered. It then searches the sub-directories, in the order they are given in the PATH statement, and tries to find a matching program in each of them.

Command Syntax

PATH=[DRIVE**][**DIRECTORY**]; ...**

Parameter Information

[DRIVE] Can be any of the physical or logical partitions on your system.

[DIRECTORY] Any directory that exists on the specified drive.

Note, you must separate each location with a semi-colon.

PATH

Command Examples

1. **PATH=C:\;C:\DOS;D:\WINDOWS** sets the path so that it includes the root directory of Drive-C, a directory called DOS also on Drive-C and a directory called WINDOWS which is on Drive-D.

Error Messages

a. There aren't any, which can be a bit of a pain because if you set the path wrongly you will never know until you try to access a program.

Notes

a. Only on exceedingly rare occasions would you include a floppy disk in a **PATH** statement.

b. If you have only one hard disk you can omit the **[DRIVE]** designator and just use the directory entries. However, it is good practise always to include it.

PAUSE

☐ Operating System   ■ Batch file   ☐ Configuration

Description

PAUSE does just that, it causes a batch file to stop whatever it is doing and wait for you to press a key before it continues.

Command Syntax

    PAUSE

Parameter Information

    There are no parameters for this command.

Command Examples

1. Where you want the batch file to halt enter **PAUSE**.

Error Messages

    a. There are none.

Notes

    a. Extremely useful for dividing batch files into small areas or to allow you to do something else while the batch file waits.

PRINT.EXE

■ Operating System ☐ Batch file ☐ Configuration

Description

This command allows you to print a file to the printer and still carry on doing something else.

Command Syntax

> PRINT [D:DEVICE] [/B:SIZE] [/U:TICKS] [M:TICKS] [/S:TICKS] [/Q:NUMBER] [/T] [DRIVE][PATH] FILENAME [/C] [/P]

Parameter Information

[D:DEVICE] The name of the print device port, i.e. LPT1, LPT2, LPT3, COM1, COM2, COM3, or COM4. The default is PRN which is the same as LPT1.

[/B:SIZE] The size in bytes of the internal buffer to be used by the command. The maximum size is 16384 bytes with a default of 512.

[/U:TICKS] The time, in clock ticks, that the program will wait for the printer to become available. The value must be in the range 1 to 255 with a default of 1. (A single tick is about one eigthteenth of a second.)

[/M:TICKS] The speed with which characters are printed, again in ticks. The value range is the same as above but with a default of 2.

301

PRINT.EXE

[S:TICKS] The period allocated for background printing. The range is as above but with a default of 8. Increasing this speed will slow down other programs.

[Q:NUMBER] The number of files that can be held in the print queue awaiting printing. The number can be in the range 4 to 32 and the default is 10.

[/T] Terminates all printing operations and removes files from the print queue.

[DRIVE][PATH] FILENAME The location and name of the file to be printed.

[/C] Removes files from the print queue. It applies to the file immediately preceding the parameter and all others following it until the command encounters a /P parameter.

[/P] Adds files to the print queue. It applies to the file immediately preceding the parameter and all others following it until the command encounters a /c parameter.

Command Examples

1. **PRINT C:\DOS\README.TXT** will print the named file using the default printer.

Error Messages

a. Error messages will occur due to mis-location details.

PRINTER.SYS

☐ Operating System   ☐ Batch file   ■ Configuration

Description

Set in the CONFIG.SYS, this device driver is used to switch code pages with different printers.

Command Syntax

DEVICE=[DRIVE][PATH] PRINTER.SYS LPT?=(TYPE[,[HWCP] [,N]])

Parameter Information

[DRIVE][PATH] Specifies the location of PRINTER.SYS.

LPT? The printer port to which the printer is attached.

TYPE The type of printer being used, one of the following:

4201   IBM Proprinter II and III Model 4201.
       IBM Proprinter II and III Model 4202.
4208   IBM Proprinter X24E Model 4207.
       IBM Proprinter XL24E Model 4208.
5202   IBM Quietwriter III.

HWCP The hardware code page, one of the following:

437   United States
850   Multilingual (Latin I)
852   Slavic (Latin II)

PRINTER.SYS

    860   Portuguese
    863   Canadian-French
    865   Nordic

n The number of code pages the hardware can support.

Command Examples

1. To load PRINTER.SYS and to use it with an IBM Proprinter 4201 you would have a line saying **DEVICE=C:\DOS\PRINTER.SYS LPT1:=(4201,437)** in the CONFIG.SYS.

Error Messages

a. Any error message will be due to grammatical errors.

PROMPT

■ Operating System   ☐ Batch file   ■ Configuration

Description

You can change the appearance of the system prompt using this command. To do so you simply enter the command name and the parameters you want to use.

Command Syntax

PROMPT [PARAMETERS]

Parameter Information

$ You have to use this sign to separate the different parameters that you are going to use, and it must precede each letter or character below. Using two dollars signs produces a single dollar sign.

B Produces a pipe character, i.e. |.

D Causes the current date to be displayed.

E Produces an escape character, actually ASCII code 127.

G Gives a greater than sign, i.e. >.

H Erases the previous character. (See below.)

L Produces a less than sign, i.e. <.

305

PROMPT

N The current drive - you normally get this by default.

P The current directory.

Q Produces an equals sign.

T Displays the current time.

V Displays the MS-DOS version number.

_ Causes the prompt to be split onto two lines.

You can also include any string of text you wish.

Command Examples

1. **PROMPT PG** is the standard prompt that you will find on the vast majority of computers. It displays the current drive and directory followed by a greater than sign. For example, **C:\DOS>**.

2. You can create some weird and wonderful system prompts by combining the possible parameters. Try this: **PROMPT D_T_THIS IS THE SYSTEM PROMPT $_$P$G**.

3. To reset the system prompt to the default, i.e. what the operating system would use given the choice, enter **PROMPT** by itself.

PROMPT

Error Messages

a. You tend not to get any error messages - but you may get some really odd results.

Notes

a. Using **PG** actually slows down the directory display because the operating system reads the disk every time you press enter to determine the current drive and directory.

QBASIC.EXE

■ Operating System   ☐ Batch file   ☐ Configuration

Description

QBASIC is a complete BASIC programming environment. It will allow you to create programs, load them and run them. As this book is about MS-DOS and not BASIC programming the following merely tells you how to start the program. QBASIC comes complete with three sample programs - try Gorilla if you like Bananas!

Command Syntax

QBASIC [/B] [EDITOR] [/G] [/H] [/MBF] [/NOHI] [/RUN] [DRIVE] [PATH] FILENAME

Parameter Information

[/B] Forces the program to run in monochrome mode even on a colour monitor.

[EDITOR] Runs the EDIT text editor.

[/G] Makes CGA monitors faster.

[/H] Forces the monitor to use the highest resolution.

[/MBF] Converts internal function.

[/NOHI] Allows the use of non-high intensity monitors.

QBASIC.EXE

[/RUN] Runs the specified program before displaying it.

[DRIVE][PATH] Specifies the location of the program to be run.

FILENAME The name of the program - which will have an extension of .BAS.

RAMDRIVE.SYS

☐ Operating System   ☐ Batch file   ■ Configuration

Description

This device driver creates a pseudo-disk drive using your computer's memory to do so. This has a number of advantages not least of which is that, because it has no moving parts, it is much faster than an electro-mechanical drive can be. Its big disadvantage is that if anything interrupts the power supply the contents of the ramdrive will be lost. You can, if you wish and have sufficient memory, create a number of ramdrives.

Command Syntax

> DEVICE=[DRIVE][PATH]RAMDRIVE.SYS [SIZE] [SECTS] [ENTRY] [/E or /A]

Parameter Information

> [DRIVE][PATH] Specifies the location of the device driver.
>
> [SIZE] The size in kilobytes that you want to ramdrive to be, and have sufficient memory for. The size can be anything from 16 to 4096. If you do not specify a size then the default is 64 Kb - which is really too small to do anything with!
>
> [SECTS] The number of disk sectors, in bytes. Acceptable values are 128, 256 or 512 with the last of these being the default. If you set the number of sectors you must also set the number of entries.

RAMDRIVE.SYS

[ENTRY] The number of files and/or directories that can be accommodated in the ramdrive. This value must be in the range 2 to 1024 and the default is 64. You can only use this parameter in conjunction with the previous one.

[/E] Specifies that the ramdrive is to be created with Extended memory. If you omit this or the next parameter, which are mutually exclusive by the way, then the ramdrive will be created using conventional memory.

[/A] Specifies that the ramdrive is to be created using expanded memory.

Command Examples

1   **DEVICE=C:\DOS\RAMDRIVE.SYS 2560/E** creates a ramdrive of 2.5 Mb using extended memory.

Error Messages

a. Grammatical only.

Notes

a. If you try to create a ramdrive that is larger than the amount of memory available then the command will make the drive the maximum size it can. This may cause problems running programs later.

311

RAMDRIVE.SYS

b. You can load the ramdrive device driver in to the HMA by using **DEVICEHIGH** provided you install HIMEM.SYS first.

c. To speed up programs, especially Windows, create a ramdrive and then use this as the TEMP directory by having a line saying **SET TEMP**=[RAMDRIVE] in your AUTOEXEC.BAT.

RECOVER.EXE

■ Operating System ☐ Batch file ☐ Configuration

Description

RECOVER allows you to retrieve data from damaged disks or files. The program reads files, sector by sector, and reassembles the data into a new file. Any data located in bad sectors will be lost. All data files that are rebuilt will be placed into the root directory of the disk that the program is being run on.

Command Syntax

RECOVER [DRIVE][PATH] FILENAME

Parameter Information

[DRIVE][PATH] Specifies the location of the damaged file to be recovered. You can recover data from a number of files by simply entering a drive letter.

[FILENAME] The name of the file you want recovered.

Command Examples

1   **RECOVER C:** will recover the data from all damaged files on Drive-C. Unfortunately there is a limit to the number of files that can be placed into a root directory and as **RECOVER** rebuilds files and places them in the root, this limit becomes the major limiting factor.

RECOVER.EXE

    2   **RECOVER C:\ALPHA\BETA.DOC** will recover just the data from BETA.DOC.

Error Messages

a. None other than generic ones.

Notes

a. You cannot use wildcard characters with **RECOVER**. You must name a specific file or else the entire disk.

b. Recovered files are placed in the root directory in the order they are found. All files will be called **FILEnnnn.REC** with **nnnn** starting at 0001 and running consecutively thereafter. You will then have to find out which files are what and rename them later.

c. You cannot use **RECOVER** on a network nor on any drive on which you are also using **ASSIGN**, **JOIN** or **SUBST**.

REM

☐ Operating System ■ Batch file ■ Configuration

Description

Short for Remark, this command allows you to place markers into a batch file, the CONFIG.SYS or the AUTOEXEC.BAT for your benefit only. Anything that follows a REM statement will be ignored as the file is run.

Command Syntax

> **REM** [COMMENT]

Parameter Information

> [COMMENT] Any string of text you wish.

Command Examples

> 1   To check the memory usage of your computer try placing a **REM** statement in front of different lines of the CONFIG.SYS.

Error Messages

> a. There are none. However, you must not use the greater than (>), less than (<) or pipe (|) symbols in the comment.

315

RENAME

■ Operating System　　☐ Batch file　　☐ Configuration

Description

Allows you to rename files but not directories. The command can be abbreviated to just **REN**.

Command Syntax

REN [DRIVE][PATH] FILENAME1 FILENAME2

Parameter Information

[DRIVE][PATH] The location of the file to be renamed.

FILENAME1 The file to be renamed. You can use wildcards to rename multiple files.

FILENAME2 The new name for the file(s).

Command Examples

1. **REN ALPHA.DOC ALPHA.TXT** simply changes the filename extension.

2. **REN ALPHA.DOC BETA.TXT** changes the filename and the extension.

RENAME

3   **REN ALPHA.DOC BETA.DOC** renames the filename but leaves the extension unchanged.

4   **REN *.DOC *.TXT** will rename the file extension of every file with a DOC extension to TXT.

Error Messages

a. You cannot have two files with the same name in the same directory. If you try to rename a file to an existing name you will get an error message saying **Duplicate file name or file not found.**

Notes

a. To rename a disk volume label you have to use the **LABEL** command.

REPLACE.EXE

■ Operating System ☐ Batch file ☐ Configuration

Description

Rather than use **COPY** to make duplicates of files you can use **REPLACE** to do so. The advantage is that you can be sure that you are really updating backup copies rather than accidentally overwriting new files with old.

Command Syntax

> **REPLACE** [DRIVE1][PATH1] FILENAME [DRIVE2][PATH2] [/A] [/P] [/R] [/S] [/U] [/W]

Parameter Information

> [DRIVE1][PATH1] The source directory from which files are to be copied.
>
> FILENAME The file definition you want to copy. You can use wildcards to copy multiple files.
>
> [DRIVE2][PATH2] The target location.
>
> [/A] Causes the program to add the source files to the target directory rather than just replace existing ones. You cannot use this parameter with /s or /u.
>
> [/P] Causes the program to prompt you before any files are replaced and/or copied.

REPLACE.EXE

[/R] Forces the command to replace Read-Only files as well as ordinary ones. Normally if you try to replace a Read-Only file there will be an error and the procedure terminates.

[/S] Causes the command to search through sub-directories of the target and replace all matching files. You cannot use this parameter with /A above.

[/U] Updates only those files that are older than those in the course directory.

[/W] Waits for you to place a disk in the source drive before the operation commences.

Command Examples

1 **REPLACE C:\ALPHA*.DOC D:\BETA /U** replaces all those files with an extension of .DOC in D:\BETA that are older than those in C:\ALPHA.

Error Messages

a. If you try to replace a file in the target directory that is Read-Only you will get an error message saying **Access denied - [filename] xx files replace**.

b. Once files have been replaced successfully you get a message saying **xx files replaced** where xx is the number of files copied. If you have used the /a parameter the message also says **xx files added**.

319

REPLACE.EXE

Notes

a. **REPLACE** is really useful for making backup copies of working files that you do not want to use **BACKUP** for.

b. **REPLACE** is another program that produces errorlevel codes as follows:

      0   Successful replace or add operation.

      2   Unable to find source files.

      3   Unable to locate path.

      5   Attempt to replace Read-Only files.

      8   Insufficient memory to carry out operation.

      11   Incorrect syntax.

RESTORE.EXE

■ Operating System   ☐ Batch file   ☐ Configuration

Description

This command is the compliment to **BACKUP**. Once you have created a backup copies of your files, you need to run **RESTORE** to reinstall the files onto your hard disk.

Command Syntax

> **RESTORE** drive1: drive2: [path] [filename] [/s] [/p] [/b:date] [/a:date] [/e:time] [/l:time] [/m] [/n] [/d]

Parameter Information

> drive1 The drive from which you will be restoring files, e.g. a floppy drive.
>
> drive2 The drive to which the files are to be written.
>
> [path] The directory into which restored files will be placed. This must be the same directory that the files came from in the first place.
>
> [filename] The name of the backed up file that will be restored.
>
> [/s] Causes the command to restore all sub-directories as well as their contents.

RESTORE.EXE

[/P] Causes you to be prompted before any Read-Only files are restored and before overwriting any files that have changed since the backup was made.

[/B:DATE] Will restore only those files that match or are older than the date specified.

[/A:DATE] Restores only those files that match or are younger than the date specified.

[/E:TIME] Causes only those files that match or have a time that is earlier than that specified to be restored.

[/T:TIME] Restores files that have a time that matches or is later than that specified.

[/M] Will restore only those files that have changed since the last backup.

[/N] Restores those files that no longer exist on the target.

[/D] Displays a list of files that match the FILENAME specified but does not actually restore them.

Command Examples

1. **RESTORE A: C:\ALPHA*.* /N** will restore files from Drive-A that came from C:\ALPHA but which no longer exist in that directory.

RESTORE.EXE

Error Messages

a. If there are no files found that match the specification you set then you will get an error message saying **No files found to restore**.

Notes

a. **RESTORE** cannot be used on any disk to which **ASSIGN**, **JOIN** or **SUBST** has been applied.

b. You can use **RESTORE** from MS-DOS 5.0 with files created by any previous version of **BACKUP**.

c. **RESTORE** produces errorlevel codes as follows:

    0 Files successfully restored.

    1 No files were found to restore.

    3 Operation interrupted by Ctrl-C or Ctrl-Break.

    4 Operation terminated due to other error.

Errorlevel 2 does not exist.

RMDIR

■ Operating System ☐ Batch file ☐ Configuration

Description

RMDIR, which can be abbreviated to **RD**, is the command that you use to remove directories. You cannot use **DEL** to erase directories - you must use this command. Any directory to be removed must not contain files.

Command Syntax

RMDIR [DRIVE] [PATH] DIRECTORY

Parameter Information

[DRIVE] Can be any physical or logical drive on your system. If you do not specify a drive then the operating system assumes you want to delete a directory on the current drive.

[PATH] The location of the directory you want erased.

DIRECTORY The actual directory you want to remove.

Command Examples

1. **RD C:\BETA** will remove the directory called BETA from Drive-C. You can issue the command in this form from any drive or sub-directory on the system.

RMDIR

2   **RD BETA** does the same thing but it must be issued from the root directory of Drive-C because BETA is sub-tended from there.

Error Messages

a. There is a single generic message that applies to this command and it is **Invalid path, not directory or directory not empty**. The message will appear if you use an incorrect path, mis-spell any part of the command or you try to remove a directory that still contains files.

b. You cannot use the command to remove the directory you are currently logged on to - for obvious reasons. However, if you try to do so you will get an error message saying **Attempt to remove current directory - [path]**. The message will also appear if you try to remove a directory to which **SUBST** has been applied.

Notes

a. Because **RMDIR** is an internal file you can use it as soon as the main operating system files have been loaded on boot up.

325

SET

■ Operating System   ☐ Batch file   ■ Configuration

Description

This internal command allows you to set operating system variables, display the current settings or remove any one of them. Normally the command is placed in the AUTOEXEC.BAT but it can also be used directly from the system prompt.

Command Syntax

SET [VARIABLE] [=STRING]

Parameter Information

[VARIABLE] Any of the operating system variables you can place or change.

[STRING] That which is associated with the variable.

Command Examples

1   **SET TEMP=D:** sets the temporary storage area to be the root directory of Drive-D.

2   **SET** entered by itself will display the current variables that are set and in force, e.g.

SET

```
COMSPEC=C:\COMMAND.COM
PROMPT=$P$G
PATH=C:\;C:\DOS;D:\WINDOWS
TEMP=C:\TEMP
DIRCMD=/W
```

Error Messages

a. Because the recognising of and the display of variable takes up memory space you may get a message saying **Out of environment space** after you issue **SET** by itself. However this is likely to happen only on machine with very limited amounts of memory.

b. Other error messages will be due to syntax or grammatical errors.

Notes

a. You would normally set all the variables you need in the AUTOEXEC.BAT, only very rarely will you ever need to set them from the system prompt.

SETVER.EXE

■ Operating System   ☐ Batch file   ■ Configuration

Description

This program loads a table of version numbers and their associated programs into memory. The version numbers are then reported to various programs. Why? Many MS-DOS programs are designed to work with a specific version of MS-DOS and while they will work with others they work better with the version they were designed for. **SETVER** tells them that they are using the version they were designed for, even though they are using version 5.0. The program must be loaded in the CONFIG.SYS before it can be used, although it can be thereafter be used from the system prompt.

Command Syntax

DEVICE=[DRIVE][PATH] **SETVER.EXE** in the CONFIG.SYS.

then

SETVER [DRIVE][PATH] [FILENAME N.NN] [/DELETE] [/QUIET]

Parameter Information

[DRIVE][PATH] Specifies the location of the SETVER program.

[FILENAME] This is the name of the program that you want to add to the table.

SETVER.EXE

[N.NN] The version number that will be reported to the program specified by FILENAME.

[/DELETE] Erases a table entry.

[/QUIET] Does not display a message as table entries are deleted.

Command Examples

1. Entering **SETVER |MORE** will display the current version table. The default table contains some twenty six program names and their associated version numbers.

2. **SETVER ALPHA.COM 3.31** adds the program called ALPHA.COM to the version table and causes SETVER to report that it is using Version 3.31 to the program. As the table is updated you get a message telling you that this is the case.

3. **SETVER ALPHA.COM /D** deletes the entry for ALPHA.COM from the table. You will then get a message telling you that the table has been updated.

Error Messages

a. As you add a program name and version number to the table you will get a long message which basically says that if

329

SETVER.EXE

anything goes wrong it ain't the fault of Microsoft!

Notes

a. You must not include COMMAND.COM in the **SETVER** table - doing so may cause your system to hang up.

b. **SETVER** tries to fool application programs by reporting version numbers to them but - be warned - this may not always work! Any problems you experience can, sometimes, be corrected by removing the corresponding table entry.

c. **SETVER** is another program that produces errorlevel codes:

0	SETVER successful
1	Invalid parameter specified by user
2	Invalid filename specified
3	Insufficient memory
4	Invalid version number format
5	SETVER unable to find table entry
6	SETVER unable to find SETVER.EXE
7	Invalid drive specified
8	Too many parameters specified
9	Insufficient parameters specified
10	Error while reading version table
11	SETVER.EXE corrupt
12	SETVER file does not support a version table
13	Version table too large
14	Error while writing table

SHARE.EXE

☐ Operating System   ☐ Batch file   ■ Configuration

Description

SHARE allows file sharing capabilities for hard disks. It used to be the case that you had to run this program if you were using partitions larger than the 32 Mb limit imposed by early versions of MS-DOS. This is no longer strictly true. For example you can safely use a 64 Mb hard disk without installing the program. The one time you really should have it installed is when you are using networks.

Command Syntax

SHARE [/F:SPACE] [/L:LOCKS]

or

INSTALL=[DRIVE][PATH] SHARE.EXE [/F:SPACE] [/L:LOCKS]

Parameter Information

[DRIVE][PATH] Specifies the location of SHARE.EXE.

[/F:SPACE] The amount of space, expressed in bytes, allocated for storing file sharing information. By default this is 2048 bytes. As this space has to include the full path to the file you may have to increase this. The default setting assumes that the average number of characters required for the path and filename is 20 bytes therefore allowing you to store information about approximately 100 files.

SHARE.EXE

[/L:LOCKS] The number of files that can be locked at any one time. By default this is 20.

Command Examples

1. **INSTALL=SHARE.EXE** included in the CONFIG.SYS will install the **SHARE** program using the default values.

Error Messages

a. Generic only.

Notes

a. If you are using any form of multitasking environment, e.g. a network or Windows, then you should install **SHARE** as a matter of course.

SHELL

☐ Operating System ☐ Batch file ■ Configuration

Description

Tells the operating system of the name and location of the command interpreter. The command is purely optional.

Command Syntax

SHELL=[DRIVE][PATH] FILENAME [PARAMETERS]

Parameter Information

[DRIVE][PATH] Specifies the location of the command interpreter.

FILENAME The name of the command interpreter to be used. Normally this will be COMMAND.COM.

[PARAMETERS] Those parameters that apply to the command interpreter.

Command Examples

1   SHELL=C:\DOS\COMMAND.COM C:\DOS\ /P will identify that COMMAND.COM is located in the directory called DOS of Drive-C. The /P makes this the permanent command interpreter.

SHELL

Error Messages

a. Generic only.

Notes

a. If you do not have a line in your CONFIG.SYS bearing the **SHELL** statement then the operating system will always look to the root directory of the disk drive you booted up from to find the command interpreter.

SHIFT

☐ Operating System ■ Batch file ☐ Configuration

Description

This command, which can only be used in batch files, changes the relative positions of replaceable parameters. You are allowed to have a maximum of ten replaceable parameters, designated by %n, and numbered consecutively. If you then need to have extra ones you have to shift the existing ones up a place so you can add the new one as %10.

Command Syntax

SHIFT

Parameter Information

There are no parameters for this command.

Command Examples

1   **SHIFT** moves parameters up a place.

Error Messages

a. There are no error messages caused by the command itself - only by its usage when you try to use a parameter that has been shifted.

SHIFT

Notes

a. Whenever you use **SHIFT** that parameter which is held as %0 will be lost and there is no way to recover it as it will have been overwritten by the parameter that was %1.

SMARTDRV.SYS

☐ Operating System   ☐ Batch file   ■ Configuration

Description

SMARTDRV is a disk caching program that holds disk information in memory. Its purpose is to speed up the disk access time so that the entire disk operation is faster. It is particularly important that it be installed if you are using any software that is disk intensive, e.g. Windows or database applications. Because it is a device driver it must be installed in the CONFIG.SYS.

Command Syntax

> **DEVICE**[HIGH]=[DRIVE][PATH] **SMARTDRV.SYS** [SIZE1] [SIZE2] [/A]

Parameter Information

> [HIGH] Loads the cache into the HMA.

> [DRIVE][PATH] Specifies the location of SMARTDRV.SYS.

> [SIZE1] The size, in kilobytes, that the initial cache will be. The size can range from 128 Kb to 8192 Kb, in multiples of 16, with a default of 256.

> [SIZE2] The minimum size that the cache can be reduced to by programs. If you omit this parameter the cache may be reduced to 0 thereby losing you the advantage of using a cache in the

SMARTDRV.SYS

first place. The size can range from 128 Kb to 8192 Kb, in multiples of 16, with a default of 256.

[/A] Tells the command to place the disk cache into expanded memory. Omitting this parameter means that the cache will reside in extended memory.

Command Examples

1   **LOADHIGH=C:\DOS\SMARTDRV.SYS 2048 1024** creates a disk cache with a maximum size of 2048 Kb and a minimum size of 1024 Kb. You must have sufficient memory available for the sizes you specify.

Error Messages

a. Generic only.

Notes

a. If you try to make the cache too large, i.e. you specify a size for which there is insufficient memory, then **SMARTDRV** will use as much memory as it can find for the initial size.

b. For SMARTDRV to use extended memory you must first have installed HIMEM.SYS.

c. Be wary of running disk compression programs while you have **SMARTDRV** loaded.

SORT.EXE

■ Operating System   ☐ Batch file   ☐ Configuration

Description

SORT allows you to input a file, sort the data it contains according to the criteria you specify and then output the sorted file to the monitor, the disk or another device.

Command Syntax

> **SORT** [/R] [/+N] [<] [DRIVE1][PATH] FILENAME1 [>[DRIVE2][PATH] FILENAME2
>
> or
>
> [COMMAND |] **SORT** [/R] [/+N] [>[DRIVE2][PATH] FILENAME2

Parameter Information

> **[/R]** Reverses the order of the sort operation so that instead of being 0 to 9 and A to Z it becomes Z to A then 9 to 0.
>
> **[/+N]** Sorts the data in the file based on the character that is in column N. If you omit this parameter then the data is sorted according to the character that is in column 1.
>
> **[<]** Directs the data from the file through the **SORT** command.
>
> **[DRIVE1][PATH]** Specifies the location of the filename to be sorted.

SORT.EXE

FILENAME1 The file to be sorted.

[>] The redirect character that allows the sorted data to be output to another file.

[DRIVE2][PATH] Specifies the location of the file that will contain the sorted data from FILENAME1.

Command Examples

1   **SORT < C:\DOS\README.TXT > SORTED.TXT** will take the file called README.TXT and run it through the sort program and then write the finished results to another file in the same directory called SORTED.TXT. This second file will be created automatically for you. (Try doing this and then reading the file using **TYPE SORTED.TXT |MORE**.)

2   **DIR |SORT** will display the directory of the current disk sorted alphabetically. If you have set the **DIRCMD** to wide format then you get something that, at first glance, looks all wrong. It isn't, it is just that the lines are sorted instead of the filenames.

Error Messages

a. **SORT: Too many parameters** is the message that will be displayed if you enter grammatical errors. You should check what you have entered by pressing **F3**.

SORT.EXE

Notes

a. **SORT** is incredibly finicky about the way that you use parameters.

b. The maximum file size you can use with **SORT** is 64 Kb.

c. **SORT** makes no distinction between upper and lower case letters and so A and a are identical.

STACKS

☐ Operating System ☐ Batch file ■ Configuration

Description

STACKS has to do with the number of data stacks that the operating system can use dynamically when handling hardware interrupts. You will probably never have to use it except on machines with odd configurations. The command must be placed in the CONFIG.SYS.

Command Syntax

STACKS=N,S

Parameter Information

N Is the number of stacks and must be in the range 8 to 64. The default on the majority of computers is 0.

S Is the size of the stacks in bytes. The value must be in the range 32 to 512. The default is 0.

Command Examples

1. **STACKS=0,0** is something that you may have to set if you run into problems using Windows and some applications. Adding or resetting this command requires that you reboot the machine.

STACKS

Error Messages

a. None.

Notes

a. I have never had to set **STACKS** - I always use the defaults.

SUBST.EXE

■ Operating System   ☐ Batch file   ☐ Configuration

Description

SUBST allows you to treat a path as if it were a disk drive. Thereafter you can use the new drive letter in place of the full path.

Command Syntax

> **SUBST** [DRIVE1] [DRIVE2][PATH] /D

Parameter Information

> [DRIVE1] The virtual drive which you will use in place of the full path. The letter you specify must not be an existing drive and therefore you may have to use the **LASTDRIVE** command first.
>
> [DRIVE2][PATH] The full path to the directory that will be substituted for by the virtual drive letter.
>
> /D Deletes a virtual drive.

Command Examples

> 1 **SUBST F: C:\DATA** will create a virtual drive, F, and then assign C:\DATA to that drive. Thereafter when you want to save data you simply enter F: in place of the full path.

SUBST.EXE

2   **SUBST** entered by itself will give you a list of the substitutions currently in operation.

3   **SUBST F:** /D will delete the virtual Drive-F, i.e. it cancels (1) above.

Error Messages

a. **Drive already SUBSTed** is the message that appears if you try to use the same virtual drive a second time without deleting it first. Each virtual drive can only have one path assigned to it at any one time and this has to be deleted before another can be assigned in its place.

b. **Invalid parameter - [?]** appears if you use the parameters wrongly.

Notes

a. You cannot use any of the following commands on any drive to which **SUBST** has been applied:

ASSIGN	BACKUP	CHKDSK
DISKCOMP	DISKCOPY	FDISK
FORMAT	LABEL	MIRROR
RECOVER	RESTORE	SYS

SUBST.EXE

b. Do not use too many **SUBST** virtual drives because each one uses memory, especially if you go beyond the point where you need to use **LASTDRIVE**.

c. You cannot use Drive-F if you have not booted your machine with a line saying **LASTDRIVE=F**, or more, in your CONFIG.SYS. **SUBST** can only use valid drive letters.

SWITCHES

☐ Operating System   ☐ Batch file   ■ Configuration

Description

This command, which must be placed into your CONFIG.SYS, forces your keyboard to behave as if it was an old 88 key TYPE – even if you are using an enhanced keyboard.

Command Syntax

SWITCHES=/K

Parameter Information

There are no parameters, the command is as appears above.

347

SYS.COM

■ Operating System   ☐ Batch file   ☐ Configuration

Description

SYS will copy the three primary operating system files to the nominated disk thereby making it a bootable disk.

Command Syntax

SYS [DRIVE1][PATH] [DRIVE2]

Parameter Information

[DRIVE1][PATH] Specifies the location of the system files, i.e. IO.SYS, MSDOS.SYS and COMMAND.COM. This will normally be the root directory of Drive-C and so can be omitted.

[DRIVE2] The drive to which the system files are to be copied.

Command Examples

1   **SYS A:** copies the three system files to the floppy disk in Drive-A.

Error Messages

a. If there are files already on the target disk you may get an error saying **Insufficient room for system files**. Use a clean disk

348

SYS.COM

instead. With MS-DOS 5.0 it is no longer vital that the system files be contiguous, or even on the first sectors of the disk, but it is certainly tidier and it does make loading the operating system that little bit faster.

Notes

a. You cannot use **SYS** with any drive to which **ASSIGN, JOIN** or **SUBST** has been applied.

TIME

■ Operating System ☐ Batch file ☐ Configuration

Description

Allows you to display or change the system time.

Command Syntax

   TIME [TIME] [A or P]

Parameter Information

   TIME is the new time to be set. It must be in the format that is set by the COUNTRY.SYS.

   [A] Specifies a.m. for 12-hour format. Whether or not you use this depends on whether you are using 12-hour or 24-hour format.

   [P] Specifies p.m. for 12-hour format.

Command Examples

   1   **TIME** entered by itself will bring up the following:

       Current time is 16:59:57.06
       Enter new time:

TIME

Just type the new time and then press **Enter**. You do not need to specify the full time, just hours and minutes will do.

Error Messages

a. **Invalid time** will appear if you use the wrong separators or go outside the range of the time itself, e.g. you cannot have 27 hours.

Notes

a. If you do not have a CONFIG.SYS and AUTOEXEC.BAT file then the **DATE** and **TIME** programs are run automatically on boot up.

TEMP

☐ Operating System ☐ Batch file ■ Configuration

Description

Specifies the location to be used for stroring temporary files.

Command Syntax

    SET TEMP=[DRIVE][PATH]

Parameter Information

    [DRIVE] Can be any valid drive of the system.

    [PATH] Specifies the lcoation of a sub-directory to be used for storing the files. At the very least you must specify the root directory by using a backslash character (\) after the drive letter.

Command Examples

1. **SET TEMP=D:\TEMP** in the AUTOEXEC.BAT sets the temporary storage area to be a sub-directory called TEMP on Drive-D.

TEMP

Error Messages

a. **Invalid drive specification** will appear if you use a drive beyond what you have got on the system, although whether or not you see it will depend on the contents of the AUTOEXEC.

Notes

a. For preference you should always use an empty directory as the nominated storage area.

TREE.COM

■ Operating System   ☐ Batch file   ☐ Configuration

Description

Displays the directory structure of a disk in graphics format (sic).

Command Syntax

TREE [DRIVE][PATH] [/F] [/A]

Parameter Information

[DRIVE] The drive for which you want the directory displayed.

[PATH] The specific part of a disk for which you want the information.

[/F] Displays the names of all the files contained in each of the sub-directories. On large disks this can take time.

[/A] Forces the command to use textual characters instead of graphic ones for displaying the links between sub-directories.

Command Examples

1   TREE C:\ |MORE will display all the sub-directories on Drive-C, 23 lines at a time. Other than on floppy disks or very small hard disk you will find that you need to use the |MORE parameter.

TREE.COM

Error Messages

a. **No sub-directories exist** will appear if you use the command with any disk or path that does not contain sub-directories.

b. **Invalid switch - [characters]** appears if you use an invalid parameter.

Notes

a. You can redirect the tree display to a file by using **TREE > FILENAME**.

b. You can send the directory display directly to the printer by entering **TREE [DRIVE][PATH] /A > PRN**.

355

TYPE

■ Operating System ☐ Batch file ☐ Configuration

Description

This command will display the contents of a file directly to the screen or you can use it to print a file. It should only be used with ASCII files or you will find some odd things happening.

Command Syntax

TYPE [DRIVE][PATH] FILENAME [PARAMETERS]

Parameter Information

[DRIVE][PATH] The location of the file to be displayed.

FILENAME The file to be displayed, and you must include the file extension.

[PARAMETERS] You can use |MORE, to display the file one screen at a time, or >PRN, to send the file to the printer, with this command.

Command Examples

1   TYPE C:\DOS\README.TXT |MORE will display the contents of README.TXT on the screen.

TYPE

2. **TYPE README.TXT >PRN** will send the file to the printer.

Error Messages

a. Generic only.

Notes

a. If you use **TYPE** with a program file you will get all sorts of odd characters appearing on screen and strange noises from the loudspeaker. You may also lock up the machine in some circumstances.

UNDELETE.EXE

■ Operating System   ☐ Batch file   ☐ Configuration

Description

UNDELETE is one of the utilities that have been licensed from Central Point Software for use with MS-DOS 5.0 Its purpose is to allow you to unerase deleted files.

Command Syntax

UNDELETE [DRIVE][PATH] [FILENAME] [/LIST] [/ALL] [/DOS] [/DT]

Parameter Information

[DRIVE] The logical or physical drive on which you want to run the program.

[PATH] The specific directory where you want to unerase files.

[FILENAME] The specific file you want unerased. You may use wildcards to unerase a group of files. By default **UNDELETE** will find all erased files.

[/LIST] Provides a list of files that can be unerased but does not actually do so. You cannot use this parameter with /ALL.

[/ALL] Forces the program to unerase files without asking for confirmation of each one. You cannot use this parameter with /LIST above.

UNDELETE.EXE

[/DOS] Unerases only those files that are marked by the operating system as being erased. You cannot use this parameter with /DT.

[/DT] Recovers only those files whose details are included in the **MIRROR** data file.

Command Examples

1. **UNDELETE** will search the current directory looking for erased files. As the program runs you will get a message saying:

   Directory: [drive][path]
   File specifications: *.*

   Deletion tracking-file not found

   [directory] directory contains xx deleted files. Of those xx may be recovered.

   followed by the first file specification.

   For each file that is found you have to supply the first letter of the filename.

Error Messages

a. **Starting cluster is unavailable. This file cannot be recovered** will appear when the file cannot be easily unerased.

UNDELETE.COM

b. **Invalid parameter specification** appears if you make an error with the program switches.

Notes

a. **UNDELETE** cannot be used to recover erased directories nor any of the files that such directory may have contained.

b. **UNDELETE** is part of PC Tools which provides a complete range of file and disk management tools.

c. Running **MIRROR** often will make using this command easier.

UNFORMAT.COM

■ Operating System ☐ Batch file ☐ Configuration

Description

Similar to the previous command but **UNFORMAT** allows you to recover erased files from a disk which has been formatted. Again this program has been licensed from Central Point Software.

Command Syntax

UNFORMAT [DRIVE] [/J] [/U] [/L] [/TEST] [/P] [/PARTN]

Parameter Information

[DRIVE] The drive which you want to unformat.

[/J] Ensures that the file created by **MIRROR** is correct without doing anything else. If you use this parameter you must not use any other.

[/U] Unformats the disk without resorting to the **MIRROR** file.

[/L] Lists all the sub-directories and files found by the command.

[/TEST] Gives an example of how the command will recreate the data from the disk but without actually doing so.

[/P] Sends messages to the printer instead of the screen.

UNFORMAT.COM

[/PARTN] Restores a corrupted partition table - provided that the program can find a file called PARTNSAV.FIL, which for obvious reasons must be on a floppy disk, created by **MIRROR/ PARTN**.

Command Examples

1. **UNFORMAT A:** will unformat the floppy disk in Drive-A.

Error Messages

a. **Invalid drive specification** appears if you try to use the command on an invalid drive.

b. **Invalid parameter specification** appears if you make an error with the program switches.

Notes

a. **UNFORMAT** is part of PC Tools which provides a complete range of file and disk management tools.

b. Running **MIRROR** often will make using this command easier.

VER

■ Operating System ☐ Batch file ☐ Configuration

Description

Causes the operating system to display the MS-DOS version number.

Command Syntax

VER

Parameter Information

There are no parameters for this command.

Command Examples

1   **VER** will cause **MS-DOS Version 5.00** to appear on screen.

Error Messages

a. There are no error messages for this command.

VERIFY

■ Operating System   ☐ Batch file   ■ Configuration

Description

Causes the operating system to check that every file write operation has been carried out successfully. As a result disk operations will be slower and so will the speed of the machine itself. However, as the command will give you advance notice of any problems it is well worth using.

Command Syntax

> VERIFY [ON or OFF]

Parameter Information

> Be definition **VERIFY** must be either in operation or not, hence the only parameter simply turns the command on or off.

Command Examples

> 1   **VERIFY ON** included in the AUTOEXEC.BAT ensures that all disk operations are checked and verified.
>
> 2   **VERIFY OFF** issued from the system prompt disables the command.

VERIFY

3   **VERIFY** entered by itself displayed the current status of the command.

Error Messages

a. There are no associated error messages.

Notes

a. With the predilection for disk intensive software I suggest that you always have **VERIFY** turned on.

VOL

■ Operating System   ☐ Batch file   ☐ Configuration

Description

Displays the Volume Label of disks.

Command Syntax

   VOL [DRIVE]

Parameter Information

   [DRIVE] Can be any valid drive that contains a disk.

Command Examples

   1   **VOL A:** displays the volume label for the floppy disk in Drive-A.

Error Messages

   a. There are no associated error messages for this command.

XCOPY.EXE

■ Operating System ☐ Batch file ☐ Configuration

Description

This command allows you to copy complete directory structures, including any files that they contain, from one disk to another.

Command Syntax

XCOPY SOURCE [TARGET] [/A] [/M] [/D:DATE] [/P] [/S] [/E] [/V] [/W]

Parameter Information

SOURCE The drive from which the data is to be copied. You must include this when you issue the command.

[TARGET] Where you want the data to be copied to. It can be a drive or path or a file.

[/A] Copies only those files that have their Archive attribute turned on. Once the files are copied the attributes are left unchanged. You cannot use this parameter with /M below.

[/M] Copies files that have their Archive bit turned on but then turns them off in the source.

[/D:DATE] Copies only those files that match or are later than the date specified.

XCOPY.EXE

[/P] Causes the command to prompt you before creating files.

[/S] The command will not copy any directory that is empty.

[/E] Copies directories to the target even if they are empty.

[/V] Verifies that each file is correctly copied.

[/W] Causes the command to pause before starting the operation.

Command Examples

1. **XCOPY A: D:\ALPHA /V** will copy the sub-directories and files from Drive-A and append them to D:\ALPHA.

Error Messages

a. If the destination does not exist or end with a backslash character then you get a message asking **Does destination specify a filename or directory name on target (F=file, D=directory)?** Press the appropriate letter.

Notes

a. **XCOPY** simply copies files and directories and so can be used to copy data from dissimilar disks.

b. **XCOPY** does not copy hidden and system files.

XCOPY.EXE

c. **XCOPY** produces errorlevel codes as follows:

   0 Files copied without error.

   1 No files found to copy.

   2 Operation interrupted by Ctrl-C or Ctrl-Break.

   4 Alternative error, e.g. insufficient memory.

   5 Hardware error.

   Note errorlevel 3 does not exist.

Appendices

Appendix 1

EDIT Operating Commands

At long last Microsoft have got round to including a text editor with MS-DOS. The text editor is actually part of QBASIC and therefore you must have this program on your path in order to use the editor.

The editor provides you with a GUI (Graphical User Interface) environment in which you can create, edit or otherwise modify pure ASCII files. The program works very much like Windows Notepad and if you have used that then you will have no problems with this.

To invoke the editor enter **EDIT** from the system prompt. You will be presented with a pretty blue screen, assuming you have a colour monitor, with a white menu bar running along the top and the cursor flashing away in the top left hand corner.

The five menus and their commands are:

File

The File menu is concerned with loading, saving and printing files. The commands, which can all be activated by pressing the highlighted letter, are:

>**New** Starts a new file. If you already have a file loaded that has been changed but not saved then you will be prompted about saving it first before the new file is created.

>**Open** Allows you to load an existing file. Activating the command brings up a large dialogue box. This is set to show

Text Editor

any file with an extension of TXT. You can change the default by simply typing a new name.

Save Writes the existing file to disk. If you are editing or creating a new file, i.e. not one that has been loaded, issuing the command will bring up a dialogue box which allows you to save the file to any part of the disk.

Save As Allows you to save loaded files to a new filename. It uses the same dialogue box as Save.

Print Sends the file to the printer. You can send selected text or the entire file. Warning: Do not try sending a pure ASCII file to a PostScript printer - you will get gibberish if you do.

Exit Terminates the text editor and drops you back to the system prompt. Any unsaved file will cause a dialogue box to appear prompting you to save the file before the program shuts down.

Edit

The Edit menu is concerned with moving text around within the file or removing it entirely. It will allow you to manipulate complete blocks of text. The commands are:

Cut Takes the selected text and places it into memory then deletes it from the file. You can then paste the cut text back elsewhere. The keyboard shortcut is **Shift-Del**.

Appendix 1

> **Copy** Similar to the above but it leaves the selected text in place. The keyboard shortcut is **Ctrl-Ins**.
>
> **Paste** Copies previously cut or copied text from the memory into the file at the current cursor position. The keyboard shortcut is **Shift-Ins**.
>
> **Clear** Deletes selected text completely. The keyboard short is **Del**.

Search

The Search menu allows you to look through files to find specific strings of text. The commands it contains are:

> **Find** Activates a dialogue box that allows you to input a string of text. You can make the search match the case and/or find whole words only. If you were to omit the latter, and ask to look at string "FOR" then the search will stop at things like FORMAT, FOREVER, FOREIGN.
>
> **Repeat Last Find** Allows you to do just that - repeat the last find operation. You can press **F3** in place of using the menu.
>
> **Change** This is similar to Find but it allows you to automatically change text strings. You input two strings, the first being the one you want to change and the second being what you want the first to be changed to. You have the option of changing a single occurrence of the target or all occurrences.

Text Editor

Options

This menu contains just two commands:

> **Display** Brings up a large dialogue box that allows you to change the display colours and generally customise the whole thing.
>
> **Help Path** Simply specifies the location of the Help file - usually C:\DOS.

Help

Activates the help system for the editor.

> **Getting Started** Brings up information of a range of topics.
>
> **Keyboard** Specific help about using the keyboard with Edit.
>
> **About** Pops up a message box with the version and copyright details of the program.

Appendix 1

Creating a file

Using EDIT to create a file is nice and simple. You have two options to start with:

1a Enter **EDIT [FILENAME]**. This will start the editor and automatically create the file you specify - even if it does not exist. However, the file only exists in memory until you save it.

1b Simply enter **EDIT** which gives you a blank screen with Untitled at the top. You can now create the file and save it to whatever filename you wish.

Once the editor is active it is simply a case of typing whatever you want the file to be.

2 Type the following, with a return at the end of each line. It is a batch file that allows you to move things around on the hard disk in one operation.

    @ECHO OFF
    COPY %1 %2
    DEL %1

3 Now save the file by pressing **Alt-F A**, which activates Save As. Press **Tab** to move the cursor down to the directory list. You can then use the cursor keys to

Text Editor

select which directory you want the file to be saved in. Pressing **Enter** with the cursor on a directory name will open that directory. Now type **MOVE.BAT** on the filename line, which is highlighted automatically when you press **Enter** to open the directory. Press **Enter** again and the file will be saved.

To use the batch file you enter **MOVE [FILENAME] [DIRECTORY]** from the system prompt. The **[FILENAME]**, which can include wildcards, replaces %1 and **[DIRECTORY]** replaced %2 in the batch file. The files will be copied from wherever they are to the directory and then deleted from the source. You can include a full path in with **[FILENAME]** if you wish and so move files from anywhere to anywhere. This is probably the most useful batch file I know of.

If you have **VERIFY** turned on then the copying process will be checked automatically for you. Otherwise you might like to include /v at the end of the copy line in the batch file.

377

Appendix 1

Changing a file

Because this is an example we are going to use the README.TXT file that is included with MS-DOS 5.0. If you have already deleted this file then use any other pure ASCII file that you have on your disk.

1. Press **Alt-F O** to activate the File Open dialogue box.

2. Press **Tab** to move the cursor to the directory list box. Use **Down** until you arrive at DOS and then press **Enter**.

3. Press **Tab** again, because the cursor will have jumped to the file name line of the dialogue box, and the cursor appears in the Files list box. Select **README.TXT** using the cursor keys if necessary and press **Enter** again. The file will be loaded for you.

4. You can page through the file using the cursor keys. As well as the standard things like **PgUp** and **Down**, you can use **Ctrl-Home** to move directly to the top of the file, **Ctrl-End** to go to the bottom of it. **End** will take you to the end of a line and **Home** will move you back to the beginning.

Text Editor

5   Move the cursor to the start of any paragraph. Press **Shift-Down**. This will highlight an entire line of text. Press the keys again and again until you have highlighted the entire paragraph. Press **Ctrl-Ins** to copy the text to the memory.

6   Press **Ctrl-End Enter**. This moves you to the end of the file and adds a blank line to the end of it. Press **Shift-Ins** and the previously copied paragraph will be pasted into place. Note that the cursor stays at the beginning of the first line of the paragraph.

7   Highlight the entire paragraph again. Now press **Shift-Del** and the whole thing vanishes. It has been copied to the memory and deleted from the file. Press **Shift-Ins** and it will be pasted back in.

8   Highlight the paragraph a third time and this time press **Del**. The paragraph is removed completely but not copied to memory. However, because you previously copied it to memory it is still there until you copy or cut something else.

Appendix 1

Searching

The text editor is very good at searching for text strings and will allow you to target what you want very easily.

1. Move the cursor back to the beginning of the file by pressing **Ctrl-Home**. Press **Alt-S F** to bring up the Find dialogue box.

2. Type **Microsoft** in the Find What box. Press **Tab** and the cursor jumps to **[ ] Match Upper/Lowercase**. Press **Space** and an **X** appears in the box. Finally press **Enter** to begin the search.

3. Almost instantly the cursor jumps to the first occurrence of the word we are searching for and it is highlighted. Press **F3** and it will jump to the next occurrence and so on.

4. Press **Ctrl-Home** to go back to the beginning of the file. We are going to change every occurrence of Microsoft to Molehill. Press **Alt-S C** to bring up the Change dialogue box. Because we have just used the Find facility the word **Microsoft** is already on the Find What line. Press **Tab** to move the cursor down to the Change To line and type **Molehill**.

Text Editor

5   Press **Tab** four times until the cursor is on **Change All**. Now press **Enter**. Too rapidly to see the file will be changed and a message box appears saying **Change Completed**. Press **Enter** to remove it from the screen.

6   Close the program down. The fastest way to do so is to press **Alt-F X**. As we have been playing with the file this action will cause a dialogue box to appear saying **Loaded file is not saved. Save it now?** If you press **Y** then it will be, if you press **N** then it won't. Then you will drop back to the system prompt.

Appendix 2

IBM Extended ASCII Character Set

On every computer that runs under MS-DOS you can access additional characters other than those which you normally get on the keyboard. These are known as the IBM Extended ASCII Character Set.

ASCII stands for the American Standard Code for Information Interchange and it is based on the original codes that were used in the days when teletype machines criss-crossed America. When computers were created it was realised that they had to have a standard system of defining characters and so ASCII came into being. The first 128 characters are identical on all computers and printers because they define the basic alpha-numeric characters and so they cause no problems.

However, the other 127 characters, which are mainly graphical in nature, are machine dependent. Those that you get on a computer are different to those that are built into printers. The result is that you can have one character on screen but you get another, entirely different, one when you print a document. (That's why the extended characters shown opposite had to be placed on to the page as a graphic.)

But how do you get these extra characters? Hold down **Alt** and then press the numeric value of the character you want on the Numeric keypad. You must use these keys and not the ones along the top of the normal keyboard. For example, if you wanted a solid block character you would press **Alt 1 9 9**. To get the square root sign you press **Alt 2 5 1**. Don't have the **Num Lock** turned on by the way when you do this.

Extended ASCII Characters

You cannot use the Extended Characters in Windows by the way. The reason is that Windows uses the ANSI character set and not the ASCII one.

128 Ç	129 ü	130 é	131 â	132 ä	133 à
134 å	135 ç	136 ê	137 ë	138 è	139 ï
140 î	141 ì	142 Ä	143 Å	144 É	145 æ
146 Æ	147 ô	148 ö	149 ò	150 û	151 ù
152 ÿ	153 Ö	154 Ü	155 ¢	156 £	157 ¥
158 ₧	159 ƒ	160 á	161 í	162 ó	163 ú
164 ñ	165 Ñ	166 ª	167 º	168 ¿	169 ⌐
170 ¬	171 ½	172 ¼	173 ¡	174 «	175 »
176 ░	177 ▒	178 ▓	179 │	180 ┤	181 ╡
182 ╢	183 ╖	184 ╕	185 ╣	186 ║	187 ╗
188 ╝	189 ╜	190 ╛	191 ┐	192 └	193 ┴
194 ┬	195 ├	196 ─	197 ┼	198 ╞	199 ╟
200 ╚	201 ╔	202 ╩	203 ╦	204 ╠	205 =
206 ╬	207 ╧	208 ╨	209 ╤	210 ╥	211 ╙
212 ╘	213 ╒	214 ╓	215 ╫	216 ╪	217 ┘
218 ┌	219 █	220 ▄	221 ▌	222 ▐	223 ▀
224 α	225 β	226 Γ	227 π	228 Σ	229 σ
230 µ	231 τ	232 Φ	233 Θ	234 Ω	235 δ
236 ∞	237 ø	238 ε	239 ∩	240 ≡	241 ±
242 ≥	243 ≤	244 ⌠	245 ⌡	246 ÷	247 ≈
248 °	249 ·	250 ·	251 √	252 ⁿ	253 ²
254 ■					

383

Extended ASCII Characters

Index

Index

Numbers in Bold denote major entries

Symbols

@	212
8086	21, 71, 73, 74, 75, 76
8088	21, 71, 73, 74, 75, 76
80186	74
80286	21, 75, 76, 85, 101, 119, 224
80386	21, 75, 76, 77, 85, 101, 103, 104, 119
80386SX	21, 76
80486	21, 75, 77, 85, 101, 103, 118, 119
80486SX	77

A

Access time	49
Active partition	239
ANSI.SYS	84, **124**
APPEND.EXE	**126**
Apple	33
Arche	118
Archive bit	139
ASCII	35, **382**
ASCII explanation	35
ASCII files	33, 167, **214**, **233**, 382
ASSIGN.COM	**130**
AT	14
ATTRIB.EXE	**133**
Attributes	
Archive	133, 139
Hidden	133
Read-Only	134
System	133
AUTOEXEC.BAT	35, 79, **104**, **137**
AUX	**40**

Index

Available contiguous memory 281
Available XMS memory 105, 281

B

BACKUP.EXE **139**
Bad command or filename 123
BAS **40**
BAT **40**
Binary Digit 43
Bit 35, 43
Boot Sector 64
BREAK **144**
BUFFERS 109, **146**
Byte 35, 43

C

CALL **149**
CD **153**
Central Point Software 282, 358
CGA 69, 214, 255, 308
CHCP **151**
CHDIR 62, **153**
Chips
   8086 .... 21, 71, 73, 74, 75, 76
   8088 .... 21, 71, 73, 74, 75, 76
   80186 74
   80286 .... 21, 75, 76, 85, 101, 119, 224
   80386 .... 21, 75, 76, 77, 85, 101, 103, 104, 119
   80386SX 21, 76
   80486 .... 21, 75, 77, 85, 101, 103, 118, 119
   80486SX 77
CHKDSK Excluded combinations **158**
CHKDSK.EXE 56, **156**

387

Index

CLS	**159**
Clusters	**57**, 246
COM	**40**
COM explanation	31
COMMAND.COM	29, 35, **160**
COMP.EXE	**162**
Computer System	
Boxes	71
Chips	73
Keyboards	71
Monitors	68
CON	**40**, 169, 174
CONFIG.SYS	35, 79, **104**, 106, **165**
Conventional Memory	100, 105
COPY	93, **167**
COUNTRY.SYS	84, **171**
CP/M	14, 16, 31
CPI files	**290**
CPU	78
CTTY	161, **174**
Cursor Keys	**20**

D

DATE	**176**
DEBUG.EXE	**178**
DEL	**181**
DELOLDOS	98
DELOLDOS.EXE	98, **183**
DEVICE	**184**, 198
Device drivers	
ANSI.SYS	84, **124**
COUNTRY.SYS	84, **171**
DISPLAY.SYS	85, **198**
DRIVER.SYS	85, **208**
EMM386.EXE	85, **103**, 115, 185, **220**, 224, 258, 281
HIMEM.SYS	85, **102**, 107, 185, 224, **258**, 281

Index

KEYBOARD.SYS	86, 113, **268**
RAMDRIVE.SYS	86, **310**
SMARTDRV.SYS	86, 110, 148, **337**
DEVICEHIGH	**184, 312**
Devices	**84**
Digital Research	15
DIR	55, **187**
DIRCMD	**191**
Directory names	**42**
Directory structure	**57**
Disks	
Access time	49
Boot Sector	64
Clusters	57, 246
Emergency Boot	186, 223, 229
File Allocation Table	64
Fitting a new one	51
Floppy disks	44, 47, 247
Logical drives	239
Partition	18, 30, 50, 53, 54, 55, 239
Root Directory	65
Sectors	48
Tracks	48
Disk Drives	
Maximum Number of	274
Disk label	247
DISKCOMP.EXE	**192**
DISKCOPY.EXE	23, **195**
DISPLAY.SYS	85, **198**
Document files	34
DOS	**200**
DOS partition	239
DOS=HIGH	107, 186, **201**
DOSKEY	**202**
DOSSHELL.COM	**206**, 232
DOSSWAP.EXE	**208**
Drive designation letters	**21**
DRIVER.SYS	85, **208**
DRIVPARM	**210**

389

Index

E

ECHO	212
EDIT	106, 214, 308, 373
EDLIN.EXE	216
EGA	70
EGA.SYS	219
Emergency Boot Disk	186, 223, 229
EMM386.EXE	85, 103, 115, 185, **220**, 224, 258, 281
Epson Extended ASCII Set	36
EXE	41
EXE explanation	30
EXE2BIN.EXE	225
EXIT	227
EXPAND.EXE	228
Expanded Memory	102
Extended Memory	101
Extended memory available	105

F

FASTOPEN.EXE	230
FAT	64
FC.EXE	233
FCBS	236
FDISK.EXE	53, 237
File Allocation Table	64, 246
File Attributes	
Archive	133, 139
Hidden	133
Read-Only	134
System	133
File names	41
File names characters	39
File names defined	37
File names reserved words	39

Index

FILES	107, **240**
Files	
ASCII	33, 167, **214**, 233, 382
Document	34
Graphics	34
FIND.EXE	**242**
Fitting a new drive	**51**
Floppy Disk	44, 52, 247
FOR	**244**
FORMAT.COM	44, 90, **246**
Formatting	
Boot Sector	64
Clusters	57, 246
File Allocation Table	64, 246
Root Directory	55, 57, 65, 246
Sectors	**45**, 48, 246
Tracks	**46**, 48

G

GOTO	**250**
GRAFTABL.COM	**251**
Graphic files	34
GRAPHICS.COM	**254**

H

HELP.EXE	**257**
Hercules	68
Hidden Attributes	133
High Capacity Disks	**44**
High Memory Area	201, 220
High Memory Area with BUFFERS	148
HIMEM.SYS	85, 102, 107, 185, 224, **258**, 281

391

Index

I

IBM Extended ASCII Set	36
IBM PC	47
IF	**261**
INSTALL	**263**
Installation	90
Intel Corporation	15
IO.SYS	28, 35, **265**

J

JOIN.EXE	**266**

K

KEYB	113
KEYB.COM	**268**
KEYBOARD.SYS	86, 113, **268**
Keyboards	71
Kilobyte	45

L

LABEL.EXE	**272**
Largest executable program	105
Laser	104
LASTDRIVE	**274**
LOADFIX.COM	**276**
LOADHIGH	268, **277**
Logical disk drive	239
LPT	41

Index

M

MD	**285**
Megabyte	45
MEM	104, 109, **279**
Available XMS memory	105, 281
Conventional memory	100, 105
Extended memory available	105
Largest executable program	105
Memory	**52**, 87
Conventional	100, 105
Expanded	102
Extended	101
RAM	87
ROM	87
Upper Memory Area	101
MIRROR	**282**, 359, 361
MKDIR	60, **285**
MODE.COM	**287**
Monitors	
CGA	69, 214, 255, 308
EGA	70
Hercules	68
Super VGA	70
VGA	70
MORE.COM	**294**
MS-DOS Versions	16
MSDOS.SYS	29, 35
MSHERC.COM	**296**

N

NLSFUNC.EXE	**297**
NOUMB	**200**

Index

O

Oxford English Dictionary 28, 43

P

Packed file corrupt error message 276
PageMaker 34
Partition 30, 53, 54
Partition Data 239
Partition Maximum size 238
Partitions 18, 50, 55, 239
PATH 81, **298**
PAUSE **300**
PC 14, 21
PC Tools 282
Physical drive 51
Platters 48
Power On Self Test 78
Primary Partition 21
PRINT.EXE **301**
PRINTER.SYS **303**
PRN 41
Program 28
Program search heirarchy 80
PROMPT 79, **305**

Q

Q-DOS 15
QBASIC 214
QBASIC.EXE **308**

394

Index

R

RAM	87
RAMDRIVE.SYS	310
RD	61, **324**
Read-Only Attributes	134
RECOVER.EXE	313
REM	108, **315**
REN	**316**
Replacable characters	**377**
REPLACE.EXE	**318**
Replaceable parameters	335
Reserved Words	
AUX	**40**
BAS	**40**
BAT	**40**
Characters	**41**
COM	**40**
CON	**40**, 169, 174
EXE	**41**
LPT	**41**
PRN	**41**
SYS	**41**
RESTORE.EXE	**321**
RMDIR	61, **324**
ROM	87
Root Directory	55, 57, 65, 246

S

Seattle Computer Products	15
Sectors	45, 48, 246
SET	191, **326**
SETVER.EXE	106, **328**
SHARE.EXE	**331**
SHELL	108, 161, **333**

395

Index

SHIFT **335**
SMARTDRV.SYS 86, 110, 148, **337**
SORT.EXE **339**
Spindle 48
STACKS **342**
SUBST.EXE **344**
Super VGA 70
SWITCHES **347**
SYS 41
SYS explanation 32
SYS.COM **348**
System Attribute **133**
System Boxes 71
System Files 142
    COMMAND.COM 29, 35, **160**
    IO.SYS 28, 35, **265**
    MSDOS.SYS 29, **35**
System Prompt 79

T

TEMP **352**
TIME **350**
Total contiguous extended memory **281**
TPI 45
Tracks 46, 48
TREE.COM **354**
TYPE **356**

U

UMB **200**
UNDELETE 283, **358**
UNFORMAT.COM **361**
Upper Memory Area **101**

396

Index

V

VER	**363**
VERIFY	**364**
Version numbers	16
VGA	70
VOL	**366**
Volume Serial Number	92

W

Windows	101, 145, 206, 219, 227, 232, 241, 312, 332, 337, 342, 372, 383
Windows Standard Mode	224
WordStar	34

X

XCOPY.EXE	**367**
XENIX	16
XT	14

PC PLUS STEP by STEP

This series, designed for clarity and ease of use, is intended for those who wish to get off to a flying start when faced with new software, operating systems or machines. These books take you through, step-by-step, the processes and functions that will enable you to maximise your effectiveness FAST. The books are written by users for users and are now published in association with PC PLUS, the UK's best-selling PC-specific magazine. The Step by Step series and PC PLUS magazine provide the complete package for all IBM - Compatible personal computer users.

Wordprocessors

Using Locoscript PC (Version 1.5)
John Campbell
0 7506 0249 X   £14.95

Using MS Word 5.0
Roger Carter
0 434 90316 7   £14.95

Using Word for Windows
Alan Balfe
0 7506 0205 8   £14.95

Using Wordperfect for Windows
Arthur Tennick
0 7506 0359 3   £14.95

Using Wordperfect 5.0
Gautier
0 434 90656 5   £14.95

Using Wordstar 5, 5.5 & 6
Alan Balfe
0 7506 0341 0   £14.95

Spreadsheets

Using Excel 3.0
Roger Carter
0 7506 0360 7   £14.95

Using Lotus 1-2-3 Macros
Ian Sinclair
0 7506 0198 1   £16.95

Lotus 1-2-3 for Windows
Arthur Tennick
0 7506 0607 X   £14.95

Using Lotus 1-2-3 Release 3
Stephen Morris
0 434 91292 1   £14.95

Quattro Pro 3
P K McBride
0 7506 0358 5   £14.95

Databases

Paradox 3.5 for Windows
P K McBride
0 7506 0610 X   £14.95

Using Q & A
Roger Carter
0 4349 0224 1   £14.95

Using Superbase 2 & 4
Arthur Tennick
0 7506 0042 X   £14.95

Using dBASE IV
Roger Carter
0 434 90251 9   £14.95

Utilities

Using Disk & RAM Utilities
Ian Sinclair
0 434 91892 X   £14.95

Operating Systems

MS—Dos 5.0
Alan Balfe
0 7506 0471 9   £14.95

Using Windows 3
Arthur Tennick
0 7506 0080 2   £14.95

CP/M Plus on the Amstrad PCW
John Cambell
0 7506 0460 3   £14.95

Machine Guides

Exploiting the Amstrad PCW 9512
John Campbell & Marion Pye
0 7506 0075 6   £14.95

Using the Amstrad PC1512/1640
Second edition
Morris
0 434 91266 2   £14.95

Using the Amstrad PCW9512
John Campbell
0 7506 0169 8   £12.95

Desktop Publishing

Ventura 4.0 for Windows
John Campbell
0 7506 0632 0   £14.95

Pagemaker 4.0 for Windows
Alan Balfe
0 7506 0634 7   £14.95

Corel Draw 2.0
John Cambell & Marion Pye
0 7506 0503 0   £14.95

Programming

Using Quick Basic 4.5
Stephen Morris
0 7506 0220 1   £14.95

Visual Basic
Stephen Morris
0 7506 0633 9   £14.95

Programming in G-W Basic
P K McBride
0 7506 0256 2   £14.95

Also of Interest

A series of handy, inexpensive, **pocket size reference books** to be kept by the computer and used every day. Their size makes them an ideal 'travelling' companion as well. **All titles are hardback.**

Newnes MS-DOS Pocket Book 2nd Edition
Second edition
Ian Sinclair

Over 110,000 copies sold of the 1st edition This best-selling title has been enlarged and updated to include material on version 5.0.

0 7506 0328 3 £9.95

Newnes MAC Users Pocket Book
Steve Heath

A handy all-round reference book for users of any MAC machine.

0 7506 0083 7 £12.95

Newnes PC Printers Pocket Book
Stephen Morris

Will be invaluable to anyone who has a program that requires them to set up their own printer codes, anyone having a problem with their printer or wants to use some of its more exotic facilities.

0 7506 0197 3 £12.95

Newnes C Pocket Book
Conor Sexton

Covers in as succinct a manner as possible the C language as defined by the ANSI standard.

07506 0221 X £12.95

Newnes Data Communications Pocket Book
Second edition
Michael Tooley

Will be invaluable for anyone involved with the interconnection of computer systems: from technicians and engineers to managers involved in the purchase of datacomms equipment.

0 7506 0427 1 £10.95

Newnes PC Users Pocket Book
Jim Reid

Based on the IBM PC range, including 286, 386 and 486 models. Will appeal to all programmers and computer enthusiasts.

0 7506 0085 3 £12.95

Newnes Hard Disk Pocket Book 2nd Edition
Mike Allen & Tim Kay

A comprehensive guide to hard disk, covering every aspect from the disk manufacture, the drives and their components, organization, utilities and data safety.

0 7506 0470 0 £12.95

Newnes 8086 Family Pocket Book
Ian Sinclair

A portable guide to the Intel family of 16/32 bit processors. Covers the 8086, 8088, 80186, 80188, 80286, 80386 and 80486 types.

0 434 91872 5 £10.95

Newnes Windows 3 Pocket Book
Ian Sinclair

Features the use of Windows 3 with MS-DOS 5, a combination which will be increasingly common as users change over to version 5.0

0 7506 0347 X £12.95

Newnes Unix Pocket Book
Heath

There are many UNIX books around but none that contain all the information necessary to get the best out of the system - This book does just that.

0 7506 0391 7 £12.95

Newnes Computer Engineers Pocket Book
Third edition
Michael Tooley

An invaluable compendium of facts, circuits and data that makes an indispensable guide to the designer, service engineer and all those interested in computer and microsystems.

0 7506 0372 0 £12.95

Related Titles...

The Chaos Cookbook
Joe Pritchard

Examines chaos theory in a much more practical way than other books and includes type-in-and-go listings which even the initiated will appreciate.

0 7506 0304 6   £16.95

Designing your systems with Smartware II
Martin Gandolf & Michael Hicks

Introduces the concepts and principles of system design and shows what must be considered when developing your own system using Smartware II. Essential for all users of the popular and powerful integrated package.

0 7506 0425 5   £19.95

Wordstar Professional Handbook Version 4
John Campbell

Provides a source of basic information while leaning and then as a handbook of practical tips and memory joggers once you have mastered the essentials

0 434 90242 X   £22.50

Using Pagemaker 3.0 on the IBM-compatible AT
Alan Balfe

Complete with appendices covering associated programs, this guide will allow you to realise and master the power and potential of PageMaker 3.0

0 434 91318 9   £16.95

Using Ventura 2.0
John Campbell

Contents: Making a Start; The basic tools; What you do - and how; Fine tuning - getting the details right. John Campbell is an experienced trainer and has the knack of covering the ground in the right sequence so that one piece of information leads naturally to another.

0 434 90272 1   £16.95

Lotus Symphony 2.0 Handbook
Stephen Morris

The aim of this book is to show you how to get the most out of Symphony 2. The emphasis is on practical applications, with examples drawn from many different aspects of business.

0 434 91302 2   £17.50

Using SuperCalc 5.0 in Business Spreadsheets in 3 dimensions
P K McBride
INCLUDES FREE DISK

Explores and explains the huge potential of the system with the 3d capabilities very much in mind. The free disk contains copies of the sheets used in the book and blank sheets ready to be tailored to your needs.

0 434 91308 1   £27.50

Hypertalk and Hypertext Programming the Interface graphic in the Macintosh and Windows 3 with Hypercard 2 Plus
A E Stanley

Presents the fundamental working of GUI in the context of object-orientated programming tools for the end user. All command/functions and uses of Hypertalk and Hypertext are covered.

0 7506 0500 6   £19.95

Wordcraft 6 Handbook
Sue Horrocks

Contents: System requirement; Operating system; Installing WordCraft; WordCarft basicsl Modes of operation; Menus; Basic text controls and commands; Using text; Designing and editing a report using advanced features; Spell check; Printing; Using images in text; Troubleshooting.

0 434 91324 3   £30.00

Macintosh Business Book
Joe Sudwarts

Written by an internationally known expert, this book covers everything from initial hardware and software selections to the effective use of networking, information exchange and communication for the Mac User in business and coporation environment.

0 7506 0502 2   £21.95

Scanning and Printing Perfect Pictures with Desktop Publishing
Peter & Anton Kammermeier

Provides all DTP users who want to integrate photos in their documents with practical hints and numerical values for image editing and printing. Aimed at the beginner as well as the professional user.

0 7506 0539 1   £36.99

Servicing Personal Computers
Third Edition
Michael Tooley

The revised and enlarged version of this bestselling book contains a new chapter on servicing 68000-based microcomputers. It has also been updated throughout and contains many new photographs and diagrams.

0 7506 0374 7   £25.00

The Scanner Handbook
A complete guide to the use and applications of desktop scanners
Stephen Beale & James Cavuoto

An authoritative and informative guide to selecting, installing and using a desktop scanner. Offers practical tips and indispensable advice throughout.

0 434 90069 9   £19.95

Wordperfect for Windows:
A Guide to Professional Document Production
Andrew Glynn Smail

Considers how to achieve predetermined goals in document production, rather than merely acquainting the reader with the use of the functions of the program.

0 7506 0541 3   £19.95

ORDER FORM

Title	ISBN	Price	Qty	Total
		UK & Surface Postage & packing		£2.00
		Grand Total		

☐ **Please send Airmail (extra costs will be charged)**
☐ **Cheques/Postal Order enclosed**
   (Cheques should be made payable to Butterworth-Heinemann Ltd)
☐ **Credit Card**   ☐ **Access**   ☐ **American Express**   ☐ **Visa**   ☐ **Diners**

☐☐☐☐☐☐☐☐☐☐☐☐☐☐☐☐   Expiry date _____
Name _____ Company _____
* Address _____
_____
Tel No _____ Signature _____ Date _____
* If paying by credit card use address shown on your credit card statement.

Please return this form to:
Alice Scott-Taylor, Butterworth-Heinemann Ltd, Linacre House, Jordan Hill, Oxford OX2 8DP.
Alternatively, phone our distribution centre direct on 0983-410511, quoting ref: B2900
(Please have credit card details ready) **PRICES ARE SUBJECT TO CHANGE**

PC PLUS

FUTURE PUBLISHING - HOME OF BRITAIN'S BEST-SELLING COMPUTER MAGAZINES - DEDICATED TO BRINGING YOU THE LATEST NEWS, PRACTICAL ADVICE, UNBIASED REVIEWS AND PURCHASING GUIDANCE TO ENSURE YOU GET THE VERY BEST OUT OF YOUR PC AND YOUR SOFTWARE.

PC PLUS - the complete package for all PC users

Over 420 pages packed with:- the latest news and independent reviews of the major hardware and software releases; 'HelpScreen' offering handy tips and practical advice; 'Programming Workshop' enabling you to program easily and effectively; the 'PC Buyers Guide' with over 1,000 listings so you can locate products, services and suppliers and, for your protection and peace of mind, there is our exclusive Buyers' Protection Scheme.

Our policy is to inform, explain, and help - rather than blind you with jargon and baffle you with acronyms. With PC PLUS, you not only get unbiased purchasing advice, you also get a whole host of features that help you to get more from your PC, improve your effectiveness, and save time and money.

On top of all this vital information, you also get a cover-mounted disk with every single issue. You can choose to receive your personal copy with either a 3.5" or 5.25" disk but, whatever the format, every disk is packed with tools, programs and useful utilities which will help you to get even more out of your equipment and software.

You gain all these benefits when you subscribe

- Your copy is guaranteed - avoid the disappointment of missing an issue.

- Your copy is delivered to your door at no extra charge - save yourself the time and hassle of having to go and find your copy every month.

- You protect yourself against inflation - the price you pay now is held for the duration of your subscription. Even if the cover price goes up, you don't pay a single penny more.

- You get first refusal on all special mail order offers we run - normally at money-saving prices exclusive to subscribers.

- You have a cast-iron guarantee. You can cancel your subscription at any time in the future and will refund you for all unmailed issues - no quibbles, no risk.

PLEASE ENTER MY SUBSCRIPTION FOR 12 ISSUES OF PC PLUS AT THE MONEY-SAVING PRICE TICKED BELOW

❏ UK £29.99   ❏ Europe £74.19   ❏ Rest of World £123.59

PLEASE TICK THE FORMAT OF DISK THAT YOU REQUIRE

❏ 5.25"   ❏ 3.5"

TO ENSURE THAT YOUR MAGAZINE AND DISK ARRIVE QUICKLY AND UNDAMAGED, ALL OVERSEAS SUBSCRIPTIONS ARE SENT AIRMAIL. THESE COSTS ARE INCLUDED IN THE ABOVE PRICES.

Name _____ Tel No _____

Address _____

_____

_____ Post Code _____

METHOD OF PAYMENT

❏ Access/Visa   CARD NO ❏❏❏❏ ❏❏❏❏ ❏❏❏❏ ❏❏❏❏
EXPIRY DATE ❏❏❏❏

❏ Cheque   MAKE CHEQUES PAYABLE TO FUTURE PUBLISHING LTD AND SEND WITH THIS CARD IN AN ENVELOPE TO THE FOLLOWING ADDRESS:

PC PLUS subscriptions, Freepost, The Old Barn, Somerton, Somerset TA11 7BR

Signature _____ Date _____

This subscription coupon valid only until 31 Dec 1992   BHFP001